Culture Keeping

Culture Keeping

WHITE MOTHERS, INTERNATIONAL ADOPTION,

AND THE NEGOTIATION OF FAMILY DIFFERENCE

Heather Jacobson

VANDERBILT UNIVERSITY PRESS • NASHVILLE

© 2008 by Vanderbilt University Press
Nashville, Tennessee 37235

12 11 10 09 08   1 2 3 4 5

This book is printed on acid-free paper made
from 30% post-consumer recycled content.
Manufactured in the United States of America

Library of Congress Cataloging-in-Publication Data

Jacobson, Heather.
Culture keeping : white mothers, international
adoption, and the negotiation of family difference / Heather
Jacobson.
p. cm.
Includes bibliographical references and index.
ISBN 978-0-8265-1617-6 (cloth : alk. paper)
ISBN 978-0-8265-1618-3 (pbk. : alk. paper)
1. Intercountry adoption. 2. Cognition and culture.
3. Kinship. 4. Mothers. 5. Adoptive parents.
6. Adoption. 7. Family. I. Title.
HV875.5.J33 2008
362.734089—dc22
2008022152

Contents

Acknowledgments

A network of people has supported, guided, and encouraged me as I worked on this book. Early conversations with Nazli Kibria, Sarah Lamb, Valerie Leiter, John Lie, Debra Osnowitz, Jennifer Ginsburg Richard, Leslie Stebbins, Stefan Timmermans, Katarina Wegar, and Kath Weston informed the direction of this project. Later conversations with Kimberly McClain DaCosta, Sara Dorow, Anita Garey, Andrea Louie, Linda Rouse, Deirdre Royster, and Beth Anne Shelton were helpful in articulating particular arguments. Conversations about it all, from start to finish, with Karen V. Hansen were vital.

Peter Conrad, Karen V. Hansen, Emily Kolker, Carmen Sirianni and Mary C. Waters provided feedback on entire drafts. Margaret Nelson and Anita Garey commented extensively on Chapter 5, another version of which appears as "Interracial Surveillance and Biological Privilege" in their edited volume, *Who's Watching? Daily Practices of Surveillance Among Contemporary Families* (Vanderbilt University Press, forthcoming). Chardie Baird offered feedback on an important section of the text. Ben Agger, Peter Conrad, Karen V. Hansen, Bob Young, and Christian Zlolniski advised me on the book publishing process.

Michael Ames showed enthusiasm for this project and

guided it from draft to manuscript. I thank him, the reviewers, Peg Duthie, Sue Havlish, Jessie Hunnicutt, and Dariel Mayer at Vanderbilt University Press for their work on behalf of this book. I owe a debt of gratitude to the international-adoptive parents who generously shared the intricacies of their lives in order to participate in my study. Without their willingness to do so, this book could not have been possible.

Heather Denning, Ingrid Furniss, Erik Jacobson, Ken Jacobson, Akiko Nakai, Toshiko Nakatsuji, Jean Neice, Roy Watt, and Susan Watt provided encouragement. Merrilee Jacobson proofread the manuscript. Caroline Gibson Florez showed interest in my work, read an early draft, and cheered me on. Emily Kolker's friendship and scholarly feedback were indispensable. Becky Barton, Evanne Gregory, Kristiina Leinonen, Sallie and Kelli McCall, and Sarah Wixson took wonderful care of Miya while I was working.

This book could not have been written without the support of my husband, Seiichiro Tanizaki, and all he does for our family. Our daughter, Miya Helen, provided much-needed distraction from the book and regular doses of humor and fun. I dedicate this book to Miya and Seiichiro. They teach me, daily, about family, commitment, and love. I am blessed to share my life with them.

Although I alone am responsible for any mistakes that follow, I thank these wonderful people for all they have done for me and my work.

Culture Keeping

1

The Call to Keep Culture

One of the first scenes of *China's Lost Girls,* a 2005 National Geographic documentary hosted by Lisa Ling, opens in Atlanta, Georgia, with five-year-old Marissa Hall, an international adoptee originally from China. Outfitted in traditional Chinese silk and red lipstick, Marissa is having the final touches put on her tinseled pom-pomed pigtails by her white mother, Denise, in anticipation of her Chinese dance recital. As Denise places the final bobby pin in Marissa's hair, she instructs, "Whatever you do, don't touch the tinsel!" reminding the viewer of the importance of the event and the labor that was expended getting Marissa properly prepared for the recital.

This small moment in Marissa Hall's life is reflective of a much larger social phenomenon that is repeated daily across the United States. Parents, most of them white, female, and middle-class, are attempting to cultivate ethnic connections for their internationally adopted children, many of whom were born in China, Korea, and increasingly Russia and Guatemala as well. Although few native-born whites have in-depth experience practicing Chinese, Russian, Korean, or Guatemalan culture, they are incorporating aspects of these into their families' lives in an effort to keep these cultures alive for their young children. By attempting to ensure that their children have access to their ethnic pasts, these parents are engaging in a process that I call *culture keeping*. Culture keeping has become standard practice within the adoption community. International-adoptive parents are often told by the adoption community that their children *should* engage in their native cultures; some are told they *must*. In adoption agency materials, on electronic mailing lists, and in memoirs, support groups, advice books, educational workshops, and conference presentations, culture keeping is framed as a mechanism for facilitating a solid ethnic identity and sense of self-worth in children who may experience difficulties because of their racial, ethnic, and adoptive statuses. Culture keeping is meant to replicate partially the cultural education internationally adopted children would receive if they were being raised within a family of their own ethnic heritage. It is meant to help mitigate some of the challenges of living in an interracial and ethnically diverse family formed across national borders.

But exactly how do native-born white Americans go about keeping culture for their internationally adopted children? And what culture is actually kept? Where do they learn about these cultures? Internationally adopted children, after all, bring little cultural knowledge with them, as most leave their countries of origin as infants or toddlers (Evan B. Donaldson Adoption Institute 2007). And young children still living at home, dependent on their parents, do not have the means with which to activate or cultivate ethnic connections independently. If those connections are to be made, it is largely up to adoptive parents to make them happen—and many do. Those parents who do keep culture find it to be important work. They speak of it as both a duty and a privilege.

Whole industries (both formal and cottage) have evolved to support international-adoptive parents in their efforts to keep culture. Online adoption shops and malls provide parents with Asian dolls, Russian Christmas ornaments, Korean textbooks, Vietnamese videos, Chinese CDs, "ethnic" home decor and toys, and much more. Vendors attend adoption conferences and workshops plying potential customers with matryoshka dolls, Chinese tea sets, silk outfits, paper umbrellas, and foreign language tapes. Travel companies specializing in what have been coined "roots tours" or "heritage tours" arrange for adoptive families to visit the countries and even the orphanages where the adoptees spent time as young children.[1] Adoptive family support organizations, electronic mailing lists, and internet groups have formed to help parents connect with one another, in part to share cultural information. Newsletters, blogs, and websites abound with recipes, holiday preparation instructions, book recommendations, and simple phrases in adoptees' native tongues.

International-adoptive parents take all this in and many take all this on, and enroll their children (and sometimes themselves) in Mandarin classes, buy Guatemalan food to prepare at home, visit Koreatown, and read Russian folktales. They attend special "culture camps" for adoptive families where they make traditional Vietnamese or Ukrainian crafts as well as participate in standard camp activities. They form friendships with other international-adoptive families with whom they have playdates, monthly dinners, and travel group reunions. They join together to celebrate Chinese New Year or Christmas with Father Frost.

This type of cultural engagement is a relatively new phenomenon. Ethnic or racial differences within adoptive families were not always viewed as incentive to connect with "birth culture" (Volkman 2003). In fact, the opposite was true. Through the 1960s, standard adoption procedures matched children as closely as possible to adoptive parents. If differences did exist—whether racial, ethnic, national origin, or religious—they were to be subverted, downplayed, hidden, and ignored. Children were to be mainstreamed—"Americanized"—as quickly as possible. The acknowledgment of difference was discouraged since the pretense of biological kinship was thought to be psychologically beneficial to the adopted child (Melosh 2002). In other words, the child was to look "as if begotten"—as if she were actually the biological child of the adoptive parents (Modell 1994). If she didn't, professional protocol advised everyone to act as if those differences did not exist.

The perspective that favored subsuming differences began to shift in the 1970s, during a time of unprecedented openness in adoption and a rise in the number of transracial adoption placements. The encouragement of cultural information and identity transmission within adoptive families began largely as a response to arguments against the adoption of black and American Indian children by white parents, who were seen as incapable of teaching ethnic and racial minority children how to contend with racism (Patton 2000, 13).

More recently, the first wave of international adoptees adopted transracially in large numbers—those originally from Korea—have begun to speak out about their experiences being raised in white communities (see Cox 1999; Bishoff and Rankin 1997; Trenka, Oparah, and Shin 2006; Robinson 2002). Adult Korean adoptees have written memoirs and poetry, and published anthologies. They have created art, performance pieces, and documentaries that highlight the childhoods they spent in relative isolation from other Asian Americans and Korean culture. These works have made visible the confusion, anger, and self-loathing they experienced due to de facto forced white assimilation.

These cautionary tales from the past have had a profound effect on how the adoption community (and industry) approaches the ethnic socialization of internationally adopted children. Contemporary adoption practices, policy, and international adoption discourse now emphasize the importance of culture keeping. The United Nations Convention on the Rights of the Child, for example, affirms that, in adoption, "due regard shall be paid to the desirability of continuity in a child's upbringing and to the child's ethnic, religious, cultural and linguistic background" (United Nations 1989). Access to the culture of one's origin is framed within this discourse as a birthright of all children.

Under this perspective of culture as an inalienable right, adoption social workers promote cultural engagement among their clients who are adopting interracially or internationally (Vonk 2001). This is no simple task. Prior to adoption, the majority of white international-adoptive parents know little about the ethnic heritages from which their children will come, beyond that which regularly circulates in popular American culture (Pertman 2000). In order to engage in culture keeping, most parents—even those who share ethnically similar heritages with their children—need to extend beyond their own understandings and experiences.

For international-adoptive parents, culture keeping can be hugely enjoyable and personally rewarding. Learning about a new culture, purchasing and consuming new ethnic goods and foods, and participating in new holiday traditions can be pleasurable experiences. In doing so, parents often connect to others on similar paths. Culture keeping can expand adoptive parents' understandings of world cultures, bring new friends into their lives, and facilitate deep feelings of connection and love for the "birth country."

It can also take large amounts of time, money, and effort. It can mean long drives into cities in order to find culturally appropriate goods or services. It can mean forgoing other activities that parents find important and cajoling an uninterested child into a cultural activity. Making these cultural connections can be uncomfortable for white native-born parents as they negotiate unfamiliar landscapes, such as Chinatown or the Russian Orthodox Church. It can be a burden to parents already loaded down with responsibilities in today's hectic world of middle-class childrearing. I first became interested in the cultural practices of international adoption in the late 1990s. I was living outside Boston at the time and saw many families around town composed of white parents with young Asian children. I saw them in white middle-class neighborhoods and in multiracial and multiclass contexts. I also saw them engaging in activities distinctly associated with China: watching the dragon boat races on the Charles River, shopping at the large Chinese grocery store, and enjoying dim sum in Chinatown. They were sometimes in large groups, wearing matching t-shirts. Often, they were alone—sometimes the parents were the only non-Asians in sight (besides me).

One day I was talking about my academic interest in adoption with an acquaintance. During our conversation, she emphatically told me that she (a white woman), her white husband, and their two internationally adopted children were a "Chinese American family." This made me pause and wonder whether other China-adoptive families also considered themselves to be Chinese American. If so, I wondered how white, middle-class parents (who, according to the 2000 U.S. census, constitute the majority of international adoptive parents in the United States) express and enact a "Chinese American" identity. What does engaging in Chinese cultural activities mean for white parents in terms of their understanding of and position in the racial schema of the United States?

During this time, I learned that many U.S. citizens were also adopting from Russia. In fact, from 1995 to 2005, China and Russia were the two largest sources of internationally adopted children in the United States (Bureau of Consular Affairs 2008a). The popularity of these two adoptive programs presents the interesting situation in which the largest international adoption programs in the 1990s and early 2000s were split over race: U.S. families with children adopted from China are largely interracial, with white parents and Asian children, while families with children adopted from Russia are mostly monoracial, with all white members. (Although both China and Russia are ethnically diverse, the children coming from these two countries are almost exclusively classified as respectively "Asian" or "white" in the United States.) How did the racial status of these children shape the rise in popularity of these adoption programs? How does both interracial and monoracial family formation shape cultural engagement among international-adoptive families? Does the support these families receive in public vary by racial make-up?

With these questions propelling my research, I completed in-depth interviews between September 2002 and November 2003 with forty international-adoptive mothers and six of their husbands in New England. In addition to conducting interviews, I observed adoption agency events, adoption conferences, and "culture days," and surveyed adoption-related websites and blogs.

The majority of the families in my study (65 percent) were composed of married heterosexual parents; however, a variety of familial configurations—married, divorced, remarried, single, cohabiting, heterosexual, and homosexual—are represented in my sample. The women and men who spoke with me all adopted their children as infants or toddlers (from five months to three years of age) from Russia or China. The children were between the ages of four and twelve when I spoke with their parents, with the majority of children in the five- to eight-year-old range. As is typical of international-adoptive parents (Ishizawa et al. 2006), all the participants in the study shared the racial and social class positions of white and middle-class, save three (one participant self-identified as both Chinese and white, and the parents in another family were identified as working-class).[2]

Despite the fact that I interviewed six fathers (and attempted to recruit more for this study), the overwhelming majority of data for this book comes from the experiences of mothers. The predominance of women in my sample reflects my study's topic. While variations have and do exist (Townsend 2002), the socialization of young children has largely been left to women in our society (Stacey 1996). Educating children about their cultural heritage and ethnic traditions are no exception. As with housework and childcare, scholars point to the overwhelming degree to which women are primarily responsible for activities related to the maintenance and celebration of ethnicity (di Leonardo 1987; Stack and Burton 1993; Glenn 1986). Evelyn Nakano Glenn notes, "Sustaining family life and transmitting cultural values is an essential part of all women's reproductive work" (1986, 15). Culture itself, especially racial and ethnic minority culture, is popularly understood in the United States to be the domain of women (Beoku-Betts 1995; di Leonardo 1987; Stack and Burton 1993; Glenn 1986). It is, in fact, often seen to be synonymous with women and is seen to reside in the "ethnic mother." As Micaela di Leonardo writes, "A large part of stressing ethnic identity amounts to burdening women with increased responsibilities for preparing special foods, planning rituals, and enforcing 'ethnic' socialization of children" (1987, 222).

Culture keeping among international-adoptive parents follows this trend. Encouraged by adoption agencies, parent-run adoption organizations such as Families with Children from China (FCC) and Families for Russian and Ukrainian Adoption (FRUA), and the growing prescriptive literature on adoptive parenting, culture keeping is posed as a necessary component of adoptive *parenting*. However, the experiences of the women in this study attest to the ways in which culture keeping is not shared by men and women but rather is experienced as a distinct *mothering* duty. This was confirmed both by the lack of interest in the study from fathers during the recruitment process and by fathers' redirecting of my requests for participation to their wives. A common response from the fathers I was trying to recruit was, "That sounds like a really interesting project. You'll have to talk to my wife!" Their wives, these men told me, would be able to talk with me about the details of their children's cultural experiences. These comments reminded me of Annette Lareau's research (2000), where she found fathers to be poor sources of concrete information about the details of the day-to-day lives of children. For example, when one of Lareau's male respondents was asked if he knew who his child's classmates were, he responded that his wife "could tell me the ones I know" (413). In my case, fathers were telling me that their wives were the best informants on activities related to cultural engagement. Although my recruitment materials purposely did not confine the project to mothers, my study was largely seen by those I was attempting to recruit as within the purview of women.

Given the range of both family forms and styles of parenting available in the contemporary United States, I am confident there are fathers who keep culture in their families. Among the six men interviewed, for example, one father was very involved in culture keeping. I also assume there are racial and ethnic minority members and those in the working class who adopt internationally and who are involved in keeping culture for their children. Data from the 2000 census, however, confirm my experience in this research project and what researchers have long speculated: international adoption is largely a white, middle-class phenomenon. While acknowledging that there are parenting variations beyond my sample, this book focuses specifically on the culture keeping experiences of white, middle-class adoptive mothers.

In this book, I explore how these women construct their families through adopting from abroad and, in doing so, construct racial and ethnic identities for their children. I am interested in how mothers themselves understand these processes, what they make of the expression of ethnic and racial identities for their children, the choices they make regarding the practice of ethnicity, and the actual labor involved. I was not seeking to test hypotheses or specific theories regarding the parenting and ethnic practices of my study participants. Rather, using a "grounded theory" approach (Glazer and Strauss 1967; Corbin and Strauss 1990), I aimed to develop a conceptual framework for understanding the culture keeping of China-adoptive and Russia-adoptive mothers.

This inductive research approach is informed by a social constructionist perspective, in that I recognize race and ethnicity not as objective facts of static biological phenomena but as ideas that have been socially created and maintained. I understand race in the United States as a changing system of socially inscribed meanings that are linked to arbitrarily selected physical traits (most especially in the United States: skin color, eye shape, and hair texture) in order to maintain power and privilege. Likewise, I view ethnicity in the United States as a concept developed socially and influenced by power dynamics. However, unlike race, ethnicity is primarily "constructed out of the material of language, religion, culture, appearance, ancestry, or regionality," rather than principally derived from physical characteristics (Nagel 1994, 152–53). Both racial and ethnic identities (and class and gender identities, as well) are constructed, "even when they go unmarked"—as race does, for example, for whites (Anagnost 2000, 390). While ethnic identification may be self-defined, racial identification is often imposed by others and reflects power relations between whites and people of color (Cornell and Hartman 1998).

The lines between race and ethnicity, however, are often blurred—especially in the ways in which people think about those categories and talk about them. People refer to someone as "Irish," for example, to signal both ethnic heritage and racial status. This phenomenon can be seen most clearly when it is challenged: for example, when someone of visibly mixed racial heritage declares herself to be Irish. Her claim to membership is met with confusion or anger by others and is often dismissed (Azoulay 1997; Reddy 1996).

Moreover, as systems of oppression and sites of identity development, race and ethnicity necessarily intersect. They are constructed and experienced (along with class and gender) in tandem with each other (Andersen and Collins 1992; Collins 1998; McCall 2005). Because of this intersectionality, how white, middle-class mothers think about culture and engage in the cultural socialization of their internationally adopted children sheds light on the experience and enactment of whiteness, mothering, and privileged social class status.

Although I argue that race and ethnicity are social constructions, I do not view them simply as illusions (see Omi and Winant 1994, 55). They are infused with political purpose and well-integrated into our social institutions. As Fredrick Barth wrote, ethnic identities are "produced under particular interactional, historical, economic and political circumstances; they are highly situational" (Barth 1994:12). As such, they can have real consequences for our lived experiences. By considering how race and ethnicity are articulated in the lives of international-adoptive families, corresponding privileges and constraints become visible.

While I am critical of the way racial and ethnic meanings enable inequality in our society, I do not intend for this project to be a critique of white international-adoptive mothers. Adoptive parents engage (or disengage) in culture keeping largely out of parental concern. They are usually engaging in practices they believe (and have frequently been told) are best for their children. I address the specific dynamics of culture keeping within international-adoptive families because they offer a window into dominant contemporary ideologies of race, ethnicity, and the family. The central finding of this book is that what mothers say about culture keeping and how they engage in it reflects larger dominant sociohistorical meanings of race and kinship in the contemporary United States. It is that larger story of race and the family that this book aims to articulate and analyze—a "story" in which we all are engaged, regardless of the racial makeup of or routes through which we have formed our families.

The following chapters follow white adoptive mothers through the process of culture keeping. I begin by situating their decisions to adopt from China or Russia within the larger picture of the "American Family." I then examine how ideas about race, ethnicity, and kinship have shaped mothers' motivations to engage in culture keeping, the pressures and constraints they face, and the content of actual culture keeping practices. I examine both how mothers themselves think about and labor to construct racial and ethnic identities for their families, and how strangers in public react to them. Throughout the chapters, I sustain a dialogue between mothers' culture keeping and how racial and ethnic meanings both constrain and enable privileges in those experiences. So while the lens through which ideologies of ethnicity, race, and family are examined is white international-adoptive mothering, this book aims to speak, in a much broader sense, to the ways in which the family as a racialized unit is produced and experienced in the United States.

2

Constructing Families

Race, Adoption, and the Choice of Country

> We tend to think of race as being indisputable, *real.* It frames our
> notions of kinship and descent and influences our movements
> in the social world; we see it plainly on one another's faces.
> —Matthew Frye Jacobson (1998, 1)

The contemporary American family is a site of kinship relations, ideological negotiations, and political confrontations.
Who lives together as a legally defined and socially recognized
family and their experiences doing so in the early twenty-first
century in the United States is not only a question of interpersonal relations and physical proximity but also of popular
ideas that frame the family as a "natural" unit. Dominant cultural ideologies of the family, although not uncontested, focus
on not only who "naturally" belongs together, which tends to
fall along lines of race, class, and gender, but how biogenetic
linkages (or the lack of such) shape relations between people.

Race and ethnicity are popularly understood in the United
States to be transmitted through families through "bloodlines": parents "bequeath" race to their biogenetic offspring.
The racial categorization of people is done differently in other
parts of the world. Omi and Winant (1994) share the example of Brazil, where biological siblings with the same parents

can be racially categorized differently based on variations in phenotype. In the United States, racial categories themselves "are based on a conception of kinship just as notions of family are based on conceptions of race" (DaCosta 2004, 25). Matters of the family in the United States have long involved race. For example, ever since the idea of "race" was constructed in the United States, concerns that surround racial boundary maintenance and the "naturalness" of racial ingroup marriage and procreation have shaped who Americans think should and who could belong together as a legally and socially recognized family. In this way, the history of race in the United States is the history of the family, and vice versa.

A central concern in racial classification in the United States has been interracial sexuality, especially between white women and men of color (Ferber 2004; Frankenberg 1993). The policing of families through legalized marriage is one of the central ways in which racial boundaries have been constructed (DaCosta 2004; Jacobson 1998; Moran 2001). This policing is visible in historic anti-miscegenation laws that were ruled unconstitutional only forty years ago in 1967 with the Supreme Court case *Loving v. Virginia*. Many Americans continue to uphold antiquated anti-miscegenation laws in practice (although not in articulated belief), as few people marry across the color line, and especially not across the black/white divide (Dalmage 2000; Davis 1991). Although the rates of interracial marriage vary significantly across racial populations,[1] Zhenchao Qian puts the overall contemporary interracial marriage rate at less than 3 percent of all marriages (2005, 3).

As this chapter will explore, dominant cultural ideas about "naturalized" kinship relations continue to shape nonbiological family formation and are evident in the experiences of contemporary adoptive families, especially those with children adopted from abroad. This chapter examines how ideologies of race and the family have helped give rise to the popularity of China and Russia as sources for international adoption and how such ideologies are reflected in mothers' narratives of their families' formation. I begin by situating China and Russia adoptions in the larger history of adoption in the United States before turning to how contemporary adoptive mothers articulate their decisions to pursue adoptions from these two countries.

Race and the Rise of International Adoption

The race of available children is, and historically has always been, at the forefront of parental "needs" in domestic adoption. Since the early twentieth century, infertility has driven "stranger adoptions" (as compared to adoption by stepparents or known kin), and white adoptive parents, who have always comprised the majority of formal adopters, have preferred to adopt healthy white infants (Zelizer 1985). (It is important to distinguish here between formal and informal adoption, for informal adoptions—often called "kinship adoptions"—have played an important role in the African American family [Kim 2008; Stack 1974]. This discussion focuses only on formal adoptions.)

The history of early international adoption into the United States diverges from that of domestic adoption. International adoption, begun in the United States at the end of World War II, was largely thought of and promoted as a humanitarian gesture (Melosh 2002). Altruism, rather than infertility, drove these early placements as Americans brought children orphaned during the war from Europe and Asia into their homes (Altstein and Simon 1991; Serbin 1997). Roughly six thousand foreign-born children were adopted between 1946 and 1953, many from Greece, Germany, and Japan (Carp 1998). Similar efforts followed the Korean and Vietnamese wars.

The plight of children fathered and abandoned by U.S.

servicemen (often called "G.I. babies" or, in Asia, "Amerasians") accounted for a large portion of children adopted into the United States. Champions of adoption such as Henry Holt (of Holt International) and Pearl Buck (of Welcome House) called upon U.S. citizens to take responsibility for these children, who were often ostracized in their countries (Koh 1981), as well as those orphaned by war, and they created agencies to match children with willing families (Conn 1996; Melosh 2002). Americans responded, and the United States soon became the "leading receiver of foreign children in the world" by bringing roughly 50,000 children into the United States from the early 1950s through the early 1970s (Carp 1998, 34).

The rates of international adoption increased in the early 1970s when a combination of social forces made the adoption of healthy, white infants progressively more difficult. Increased access to birth control, the legalization of abortion in 1973 with *Roe v. Wade,* a lessening of the stigma around single parenthood, and an increase in the stigma around infant relinquishment resulted in a drop in the numbers of white women relinquishing their (white) infants for adoption (Bagley 1993; Melosh 2002; Mundy 2007; Pertman 2000; Simon and Altstein 1992; Solinger 2001).

While some prospective adopters sought white babies through privately arranged adoptions or chose to adopt older white children with physical or psychological disabilities, the dwindling supply of healthy white infants had some prospective adopters turning to the domestic transracial adoption of black, biracial, or American Indian children. Prior to the 1950s, formal transracial adoption was rare, due to social attitudes against interracial families, legalized racial segregation, and the explicit adoption practice that sought to "match" children with parents along the lines of race, ethnicity, religion, and even temperament and personality (Melosh 2002). In the wake of the civil rights movement and changing race rela-

tions and racial attitudes—and the scarcity of white infants—
adoption agencies began to place available minority children
in white homes (Carp 2002; Freundlich 2000). The number of
these transracial domestic adoptions, however, remained small;
social historian Barbara Melosh puts these adoptions at "no
more than 2 or 3 percent of all adoptions even at their peak in
1971" (2002, 159).

Despite the small numbers, the domestic adoption of children of color by whites in the United States has been severely
contested and hotly debated. Central to this debate is concern
over the psychological and emotional outcomes of such adoptions and the impact they have on both children and communities of color. Starting in the early 1970s, the ability of whites
to shape healthy racial and ethnic identities for their adopted
black children was publicly questioned. In 1972, the National
Association of Black Social Workers (NABSW) issued a statement that argued against domestic transracial adoption on the
grounds that white adoptive parents were incapable of "teaching their Black children how to resist and undercut potentially devastating and ubiquitous racial stereotypes and racist ideology" (Patton 2000:13). As Laura Briggs (2005) writes,
in calling for a moratorium on transracial placements, the
NABSW was arguing for the preservation of African American families at a time when those families were largely characterized, via the Moynihan Report (1965), as a "tangle of pa-
thology." The NABSW proposed that "black children should
be placed only with black families whether in foster care or
adoption. Black children belong physically, psychologically,
and culturally in black families in order that they receive the
total sense of themselves and develop a sound projection of
their future" (Silverman 1993, 106).

While transracial adoptions did not end, they were curtailed. In 1973, the formal adoption standards of the Child
Welfare League of America were changed, giving preference to

monoracial placements over transracial ones (Herman 2005). The Multiethnic Placement Act of 1994 (amended in 1996) now prohibits "the use of a child's or a prospective parent's race, color, or national origin to delay or deny the child's placement" (Hollinger 2005), but the rates of domestic transracial adoptions remain low (Melosh 2002).

Similar to the debate over the transracial adoption of black children by whites, the transfer of American Indian children from their natal families to whites has undergone intense scrutiny and change. The removal of American Indian children from reservations has a long and complex history. From the 1880s to the 1950s, American Indian children were forcibly removed from their homes and placed in white-run boarding schools (George 1997) for the "purposes of education and 'civilization'" (Freundlich 2000, 58). Starting in the 1950s, the "Indian Adoption Project" removed American Indian children from their families over concerns about child safety and protection. The children were adopted into white homes or placed in white-run institutions. Social workers saw American Indian parenting practices as neglectful and harmful to children and transferred children to white middle-class homes where they felt the children would receive better care (Fanshel 1972).

Although social workers were following professionally defined protocol, it has been argued that the Indian Adoption Project was, in effect, "simply carrying on with the detribalization of Native Americans begun by the federal government" during the 1800s (Sindelar 2004, 2). According to the Association of American Indian Affairs (AAIA), by the late 1960s, "one in four Indian children in states with significant Native populations" had been removed from their families and placed in "foster, adoptive, or institutional care" (Briggs 2005, 5). Beginning in the late 1960s, American Indian activists began to vocally protest this "detribalization" via the forced removal of their children (Briggs 2005). They argued for family preservation and tribal self-determination (George 1997). In 1978, the Indian Child Welfare Act (ICWA) gave Indian tribes exclusive jurisdiction "over any child custody proceeding involving an American Indian child" (U.S. Congress 1978). It is difficult to ascertain the impact of the ICWA and the NABSW's calls to end transracial adoption on international adoption rates. However, it was in the context of those debates and, perhaps more importantly, the scarcity of white infants, that increasing numbers of people began looking overseas for children.

Adopters, however, were not only "pushed" overseas, they were "pulled" there as well through constructions of desire for particular kinds of children to fulfill particular kinds of families. Racial preference, in particular, shaped the increasing popularity of international adoption. The majority of children who have been adopted internationally into the United States have been Asian (Kreider 2003; Bureau of Consular Affairs 2008a). While these children are nonwhite, they are also nonblack. It has been strongly argued that it was not only a desire for infants that pulled potential adopters overseas, but a desire to avoid the adoption of a black child (Dorow 2006b; Kim 2008; Rothman 2005).

The adoption of Asian children by white parents is facilitated by the fact that acceptance of Asian/white interracial families has increased. While inequality structures the lives of many Asians in the United States, particularly for recently arrived groups, the stigma of white/Asian interracial families, historically severe, has lessened during the last several decades in ways that it hasn't for black/white families (Fryer 2007; Rothman 2005). This can be seen when comparing contemporary patterns in interracial marriage. Asian Americans and Latinos are the groups most likely to intermarry with whites;

African Americans are the least likely to do so (Batson, Qian, and Lichter 2006; Feliciano 2001; Lea and Bean 2004; Perlmann 2000). From the 1970s to the 1990s, as increasing numbers of adopters began to look overseas for their children, international adoption became big business. Within the international adoption industry, an uneven distribution of power and resources—both within countries and between them—can be seen. Globally, international adoption pulls children from certain parts of the world—namely, ones that are largely poor and darker-skinned—and places them in other parts, ones that are largely wealthy and lighter-skinned (Herrmann and Kasper 1992).[2]

This has influenced which countries begin and which sustain adoption programs. Countries that open their borders to international adoption often do so as a stopgap measure to help address the issue of children abandoned or orphaned due to economic strife, poverty, political instability, war, or social upheaval. But as demographer Peter Selman notes, it is "evident that the major sources [for international adoption] have not been the poorest or highest birth rate countries, that patterns persist long past the 'crisis' and that demand for children is also a key factor" (2002, 218). International adoption from Korea, which has been extremely popular in the United States, is a good example.

It is estimated that, from the period following the Korean War through the 1980s, more than 100,000 children left Korea to be adopted by families in the Western hemisphere (Altstein and Simon 1991). Korean adoptions began as a response to the overwhelming number of children in state care following the Korean War. However, even as the economy of Korea began to recover from the devastation of the war and eventually prosper, and even as the Korean government grew sensitive to international adoption and began restricting placements,[3] children continued to leave the Korean peninsula to be adopted by Westerners (Altstein and Simon 1991; Freundlich 2000). In the late 1980s alone, the annual number of children being adopted out of Korea was "6,500–9,000 cases a year, representing an amazing 1–1.4 percent of the country's annual living births" (Hübinette 2004). The Korean example shows that, as international adoption shifted to a business model, the industry itself, driven by profit and the needs of would-be adopters for particular kinds of children (i.e., young, available, and nonblack), has influenced which programs (i.e., countries) become popular and which are sustained even beyond the crisis from which they originated.

Contemporary International Adoption from China and Russia

In the early 1990s, international adoption rates began a dramatic climb. In the decade from 1995 to 2005, the total number of international adoptions increased 150 percent, from a total of 8,987 to 22,728 children brought into the United States (Bureau of Consular Affairs 2008a). During this period, China and Russia accounted for roughly half of all international adoptions and were the top two countries from which children were adopted (see table); China led in adoptions, except for the years 1997, 1998, and 1999, when Russia was the leading country.[4] The dramatic increase in international adoptions since the early 1990s can, therefore, be linked to the opening of China and Russia as new adoption programs for international placements.

China and Russia officially opened to international adoption in the early 1990s during a time of increased child abandonment in these two countries. The reasons behind the rising numbers of children in state care in China and Russia differ. In Russia, as in many countries, poverty, family violence, disease

Number of Immigrant Visas Issued to Adopted Children from 1990–2007

Year	Total	Russia	China	Largest	Second Largest
1990	7,093	—	29	Korea (2,620)	Colombia (631)
1991	8,481	—	61	Romania (2,594)	Korea (1818)
1992	6,472	324	206	Korea (1,840)	Guatemala (418)
1993	7,377	746	330	Korea (1,775)	Russia
1994	8,333	1,530	787	Korea (1,795)	Russia
1995	8,987	1,896	2,130	China	Russia
1996	10,641	2,454	3,333	China	Russia
1997	12,743	3,816	3,597	Russia	China
1998	15,774	4,491	4,206	Russia	China
1999	16,369	4,348	4,101	Russia	China
2000	17,718	4,269	5,053	China	Russia
2001	19,237	4,279	4,681	China	Russia
2002	20,099	4,939	5,053	China	Russia
2003	21,616	5,209	6,859	China	Russia
2004	22,884	5,865	7,044	China	Russia
2005	22,728	4,639	7,906	China	Russia
2006	20,679	3,706	6,493	China	Guatemala (4,135)
2007	19,613	2,310	5,453	China	Guatemala (4,728)

Source: All data are from the U.S. Department of State (Bureau of Consular Affairs 2008a).

(including HIV), difficulties in obtaining contraception, crime (including that committed by children), and the effects of alcohol and drug addiction play a large role (Harwin 1996). In particular, economic instability (including high rates of unemployment) and dramatic social changes since the fall of Communism have had dire consequences for families, with more Russian parents having to relinquish their children—either voluntarily or by court order—due to their inability to care for them (Harwin 1996; Steltzner 2003). Child neglect, resulting in more than 100,000 children *yearly* being registered with the state, has been cited as "one of the problems in Russian society causing most serious concern" (Zbarskaya 2001, 34). Both boys and girls are being relinquished or abandoned in Russia, which contrasts with China, where roughly 98 percent of the children adopted out are girls who were abandoned in infancy or toddlerhood (Miller-Loessi and Zeynep 2001).[5]

It is widely reported that the abandonment of children in China—girls in particular—occurs mainly because of the effects of a series of state regulations begun in the 1970s (Tessler, Gamache, and Liu 1999). Meant to restrict the expansion of China's population, the most extreme of these fertility policies was implemented in 1980 and is referred to as the "one-child policy" (Feng 2005). The enforcement of these fertility policies,[6] which became stricter in the late 1980s, coupled with the cultural preference for sons,[7] resulted in a sharp increase in child abandonment, female infanticide, and sex-selective abortion (Johnson et al. 1998; Li 1995). The widespread practice of these acts can be seen in the resulting imbalanced sex ratio in China. While normal birth sex ratios worldwide average 106 males to every 100 females (Zeng et al. 1993), in 2000 China's was 116.8 males to every 100 females (Liu et al. 2004).

It is reported that children in China are usually abandoned in infancy in relative secrecy. They are often left in public places where, it is assumed, they are intended to be discovered quickly. The abandonment of children in China is illegal, although not often punished (Johnson et al. 1998). This contrasts with Russia, where strict abandonment laws do not exist, and where infants are left at birth in hospitals and children of all ages are abandoned, formally relinquished, or taken into state care.

As the numbers of children in state care in Russia and China began to mount in the late 1980s, international adoption became a vehicle through which the increasing demands for their care were addressed. China instituted its first adoption law in 1991. This law standardized and regulated both domestic and international adoption within China (National People's Congress 1991).

As adoption became more formalized in China, it actually became increasingly difficult for Chinese citizens to adopt. In particular, the requirement that adopters be at least thirty-five years of age and childless severely limited the numbers of Chinese able to adopt. Kay Johnson, Haung Banghan, and Wang Liyao speculate that this law was not intended to help find homes for the many needy infants in state care but rather "to prevent birthparents from arranging adoptions for 'excess' daughters so as to be able to try again for a son" (1998, 478). Although the new adoption laws curtailed domestic adoption, they did pave the way for international adoption. The Chinese government welcomed foreigners as one way to help restrict the growing numbers of children in orphanages (Johnson et al. 1998).

Adoption in China is a highly regulated process overseen by the China Center for Adoption Affairs (CCAA). This contrasts with the situation in Russia. In 1990, the Soviet Union signed the United Nations Convention on the Rights of the Child, which led to the opening of the country for international adoption (Saidazimova 2005). While the Ministry of Education and Science of the Russian Federation oversees orphanages in Russia, there has been no central adoption authority equivalent to the CCAA (Harwin 1996).[8] District courts oversee international adoptions in Russia, and procedures can (and do) vary regionally and locally (Erichsen and Erichsen 2003). This is important to note as it influences the process through which international-adoptive parents must traverse to receive their children in each country.

The international adoption process requires parents to be

very specific about what kind of child they would like to adopt in terms of age, race, ethnicity, disability, sibling group, and gender. These criteria direct parents to particular agencies and to particular countries. Once prospective adopters have selected an agency and program, they must be approved for adoption by a licensed social worker, receive clearance from the office of the United States Citizenship and Immigration Services (USCIS, formerly the Immigration and Naturalization Services [INS]), and fill out reams of paperwork. With the assistance of their agency, they send their paperwork file— their "dossier"—to their country of choice. They then wait for the "referral" of a child for adoption. If they agree to the referral, they travel to the country to pick up the child (or await her arrival in the United States) and complete the adoption (Rojewski and Rojewski 2001).

This is the general process of all international adoptions, although the particulars can vary widely from country to country. These variations in the adoption process play a role in both the parental choice of an adoptive country and, later, in the development of adoption communities in which culture keeping occurs.

The China adoption program is unique in that parents most often travel in groups (organized by their U.S. adoption agencies) to meet and collect their children. (In the early years of China adoption, some families, including several in my sample, traveled alone.) The time spent in China varies, but an average trip usually entails several weeks (Bureau of Consular Affairs 2006). Translators and guides are often provided by the agencies, and some sightseeing arranged as well. While in the past adopters were regularly allowed to visit orphanages or foster families, this practice was halted following the airing of *The Dying Rooms,* a BBC documentary that critically portrayed Chinese orphanages, angering Beijing. Although restrictions to orphanages have since loosened, children are usually brought to their new parents, with the first meeting often occurring in the hotel in which the parents are staying. The family then remains in-country while various documents are processed and the child is cleared for international travel.

Parents who adopt from Russia must follow the same procedures as parents who adopt from China (sending a dossier, waiting for a referral, and traveling to the country to pick up the child and formalize the adoption). However, Russia-adoptive families most often travel alone or meet up with one or two other families in Russia; they do not travel as an organized group. The time spent in-country does not usually include a formal schedule of sightseeing, although this is beginning to change, with some recent Russia-adoptive parents reporting more organized itineraries. Adopters in Russia sometimes lodge with Russian host families (arranged by their adoption agencies), while those in China stay exclusively in hotels. While foreigners are now required to make two trips to Russia in order to procure an adoption, the parents in my study, who all adopted in the 1990s, only had to make one trip.

Adopting a child internationally requires a great deal of planning, paperwork, and patience on the part of prospective adopters. The process of adopting from China and Russia was quite similar from the inception of their international adoption programs through the 1990s, especially as compared to other international adoption programs that required, for example, extended stays in-country.

Given the larger historical context of biogenetic and race ideologies in the understandings of "family," how do women articulate their decision to adopt? How do they come to and narrate the "choice" of China or Russia? Through examining the criteria along which white adoptive mothers construct their families, the larger ideology of the family as a racialized unit becomes visible.

Adoption Decisions

People who decide to adopt their children from abroad often follow a common trajectory. Many, such as thirty of the forty women who spoke with me, experience primary or secondary infertility or pregnancy loss and attempt high-tech fertility treatment before turning to adoption as a way to parent.[9] In a society that commonly views "fertility [as] the norm" in which "children symbolize the re-creation of the self and the future—the continuity of the family, the march of generations, the renewal of life" (Becker and Nachtigall 1991, 876), grief over infertility is seen as a necessary part of forming a nonbiological family. People working in the field of adoption speak of a grieving process prospective adopters must undergo as they move through each stage and come to terms with the fact that they will be unable to bear a child physically with whom they share a biogenetic connection. Adoption experts have long argued that moving through this grief is both healthy and necessary. They encourage people, especially women, to engage in this emotional work (see Johnston 1992; Sorosky, Baran, and Pannor 1978; Steinberg and Hall 2000).

In my interviews, I found women speaking of this process in a more varied way than one would have surmised from adoption grief literature. Some women described this process as relatively easy. Emma Moore,[10] for example, told me that after she and her husband married, "we tried to start a family but were not able to do so. And [my husband] felt similarly to myself and we both wanted to become parents; that was the important thing. We were totally okay with adoption. It wasn't sort of a struggle to get to that point. We gave it a good try, we weren't able to have a biological child with some medical assistance, and we moved on from there."

Emma did not undergo the extended grieving process advised by adoption experts. She was not wedded to the idea of the biogenetic family. She and her husband relatively quickly moved on to adoption following a brief unsuccessful foray into the world of reproductive technologies. Other women also spoke of this process as one that contained little grief for them.

More commonly, however, women spoke of an emotional struggle with infertility and a grief they experienced for the biological child they were unable to conceive or bear. These women, if they had the money and stamina, pursued more intensive and invasive forms of reproductive assistance (see also Mundy 2007; Orenstein 2007), although none in my sample did so with success. Jamie Naylor shared with me the various avenues through which she and her husband tried to have a biologically related child. Characterizing it as "quite a process," she told me, "We went through some pregnancy loss. We attempted alternative, more high-tech ways to become birth parents and I was not ready to think of adoption until that card hand was played out fully."

In the late 1980s and early 1990s, "fully playing out" the assisted reproduction card meant pursuing in vitro fertilization (IVF). While one billion dollars was spent annually on infertility treatments by the late 1980s (Solinger 2001, 204), success rates at the time for IVF (evidenced by live births per IVF cycle) were estimated from only 6 to 10 percent (Bartholet 1999, 208; Mundy 2007, 31).[11] By the early to mid-1990s, when many women in my study were attempting to get pregnant, the average time spent in infertility treatment was three years or more, with some people reportedly investing up to five or ten years trying to reproduce (Becker and Nachtigall 1994). The Centers for Disease Control (CDC) estimated that the success rate for live births per assisted reproductive technology (ART) cycle (IVF, GIFT, and ZIFT) in 1995 was just under 20 percent (1997, 11).

As with unassisted reproduction, success rates for assisted

reproduction also decline with age. The same CDC report stated that only 7 percent of ART cycles on forty-two-year-old women (the average age at which women in my study adopted) resulted in live births (CDC 1997, 15). In her recent book on assisted reproduction, Liza Mundy reports, "Studies show that among ART patients who are forty years old and using their own eggs, there is a 25 percent chance of pregnancy over the course of three IVF cycles. The chances diminish to around 18 percent at forty-one and forty-two, 10 percent at forty-three, and 0 at forty-six" (2007, 42).

The experience of Eloise Nolan, who did attempt IVF before adopting twice from China, was typical of women in my study who tried to get pregnant through ART. Eloise spoke of the futility she'd felt:

> We never even had a fertilized egg. So the physician I had was very good and said, "Don't waste any more of your money." Because by that time I was forty and he said, "Your chances are nil." He said, "I'll just keep doing it if you want me to," but we had to pay up front because insurance didn't cover for IVF and it's about $10,000 a shot. It was becoming useless.

While infertility and disappointment with ART bring many to adoption, there are adoptive parents (such as ten who spoke with me) who pursue adoption as their first preferred route for family expansion. Some of these are single women or partnered lesbians who bypass pregnancy because they do not want to use high-tech fertility treatment or the "known-donor" route to becoming a mother. Others are heterosexually partnered women who purposely avoid pregnancy.

Many "first choice" adopters begin to contemplate adoption in adolescence or early adulthood. This was the case with Jean Kerne, a Russia-adoptive mother, who explained that she'd known her preference since her early twenties: "That's how I wanted to have a family. I wasn't interested in the birth process . . . genetic connection didn't mean all that much to me. I wanted to be a mom. But I wanted to adopt."

Preferring adoption over pregnancy as a route to parenthood is an unconventional choice in our reproduction-focused society (Hertz 2006; Morris 1999). Women who bypassed reproduction from the outset understood this. They spoke of having to manage an assumption of infertility and "second best" adoption. Indicative of this were uncomfortable or humorous exchanges with friends, colleagues, and acquaintances who commiserated over failed reproduction. Leanne Becker, who along with her husband adopted two girls from China, spoke of how the assumption of infertility infiltrated conversations she had once her adoption plans were made public:

> I know that most people just assumed that we were having fertility problems that I had never spoken about. Because people would say things sometimes about, "Oh just wait. As soon as you get that first baby, you'll get pregnant." And I was like, "Gosh, I hope not. It would be really inconvenient. We're going to do our best to make sure that doesn't happen." [*laughter*]

Those who choose adoption from the outset spoke of doing so in order to fulfill two needs ideally and complementarily: their own desire to parent and a child's desire for a family. In their articulated motivations to adopt from overseas, these "first choice" adopters echo the humanitarian impulse that had characterized the framing of international adoption in the first half of the twentieth century. "Child-saving," however, is no longer totally accepted in the larger adoption community as an appropriate motivation for bringing a child into one's home.[12] Narratives of rescue hide how power and privilege have influenced which mothers have been able to raise the children they bear and which have been able to adopt (Patton 2000; Roberts 2003). Adult international adoptees have argued that narratives of rescue cast sending countries, cultures, and families as essentially negative and receiving countries as essentially positive (see Kim 2007). Some argue that adoption as rescue reeks of colonialism, glosses over parental desire, and places too much pressure on adoptees to be grateful for having been "saved." A taboo of rescue can be seen in my own research, in that many women who expressed a humanitarian impulse to adopt were also quick to voice their own desire to parent. With humanitarianism no longer operating as the dominant framing for international adoption, and with many children in state care in the United States, how do mothers narrate choice in their adoption stories?

Going Abroad

The adoption stories of international-adoptive mothers often follow a narrative structure that contains the answers to two questions: Why adoption? And why x country (e.g., Russia or China or Guatemala)? This same narrative structure can be seen in the many adoption memoirs and popular press articles written by academics, journalists, and creative writers who are themselves adoptive parents. Writing in *The Boston Globe*, adoptive mother Janice Page spoke of these two questions:

> Especially if it's your first child, people typically want to know what made you decide to adopt (translation: couldn't you give birth?) and why you chose to adopt from China. Given that there are more than 125,000 foster-care children awaiting adoption in the United States, as well as countless other abandoned children around the globe, that last question is as understandable as it is loaded.

While I would argue that both of these questions are actually "loaded," as the first casts adoption as nonnormative ("couldn't you give birth?") and the second as suspect (why didn't you adopt one of the "125,000 foster-care children awaiting adoption in the United States?"), it is in answering the second question that ideologies of race and the family become articulated. According to my respondents, the decision to adopt a child internationally rather than domestically is propelled by a combination of several factors. Racial and kinship preferences, however, dominate that choice. Important in this discussion is the structure of domestic adoption. Domestic (formal) adoptions occur through the state or privately through for-profit agencies, lawyers, or nonprofit agencies. These variations are important, particularly the state vs. private distinction, as the salient differences between state and private adoptions for the women in my sample were: 1) the ages, histories, and race of available children, and 2) adoption procedures. Private adoptions most often involve newborns, with the birth parent(s) frequently involved in the selection of the adoptive family. State adoptions most often involve older children, many of whom have experienced some type of trauma (e.g., neglect, abuse, removal from birth family, or foster care placement) (Freundlich 2000; Rothman 2005). While white and minority children are available in both private and state adoptions, very few white newborns can be adopted through the state.

The possibility of adopting domestically largely went unmentioned in the adoption stories shared with me. Only one woman had previously adopted domestically (through the state). Several women mentioned the possibility of a domestic placement, but most were referencing private, not state, placements. It was as if domestic adoption was completely off the radar in the decision-making process. Most women leapt from stories of infertility to international adoption programs when discussing their plans to adopt. This speaks to the popularity of international adoption and its increasing institutionalization among prospective adopters.

In this disregard for domestic adoption, particularly state adoptions, a preference for particular kinds of children and particular kinds of adoption experiences can be seen. The subtext of this preference was the avoidance of older, (assumingly) troubled, black or biracial children and a privileging of healthy, and (presumably) unencumbered white or Asian infants. Katherin M. Flower Kim notes this as well in her study of Korea-adoptive parents. She writes, "For most parents, 'domestic' adoptions were understood and coded almost exclusively as the search for healthy, *white* infants" (2008, 396). This is not surprising given the historical preference for white infants in formal adoption in the United States.

The women in my study explained to me that they avoided adopting black children because of the negative reactions they anticipated receiving from friends and family. Eloise Nolan, for example, felt that the adoption of a black child would have sent her family members "through the roof" and she "didn't want to create any kind of family conflict." Participants also framed the domestic transracial adoption of black children by whites as "unfair" because of the racial prejudice the children would face. Leanne Becker's comments were emblematic of this perspective: "Children have a hard enough time facing what they face outside the family. They need to have total acceptance inside the family."

This idea of "total acceptance in the family" for the child facilitated by race was the framing for much of the adoption decision-making. The parents who adopted from Russia were quite explicit that they wanted to adopt a Caucasian child who looked similar to themselves because the child would be more easily accepted into the family. Likewise, the majority of China-adoptive parents did not consider adoption from Asia problematic. While several participants noted open hostility within their extended family regarding the adoption of a Chinese child, most reported a familial acceptance of Asians. Although Eloise Nolan was confident that the adoption of a black child would have been a polarizing event in her extended family, she noted that "nobody had any problem with Asians. It was like, so, everyone was very supportive. Both families helped us financially as well and everyone was ecstatic. It was great." According to study participants, that fact that family and friends believed Asians to be the "model minority" (possessing special qualities such as being studious, intelligent, well-mannered, family-focused, economically independent, and resourceful, setting them apart qualitatively from other racial and ethnic minorities) sold them on Chinese adoption. Holly Pritchard felt that her parents would have opposed the adoption of a black child but were content with a Chinese adoption because "as much as they love my daughter, [they] had very stereotypical ideas about what she would be like. [They] assumed she would be smart; assumed—you know, all these things, because that's their—the stereotypical view. And from that perspective it's made it easier, but sometimes I realize how unrealistic that really is, too."

Because of this bias against black children (who participants understood to be overrepresented in the state system), if domestic adoption was to be pursued seriously, the parents in my study only considered private adoption.

Yet private adoption itself was fraught with various perils to the particular type of kinship that women wanted to construct with their adopted children. They wanted an exclusive relationship with their child that did not involve birth parents. An important stumbling block to this desired kinship for many was the fact that in contemporary private domestic adoption, birth mothers are often involved. Commonly, this involvement begins with birth mothers selecting the families they would like to raise their children. The adoptive mothers in my study believed that certain characteristics they held (such as those related to advanced age, religion, disability, or divorce) would have made them less attractive to birth mothers. Because she belonged to a religious minority, Emma Moore felt, "very resentful about the whole way that adoption is handled in the U.S." She went on: "You want to adopt a baby and the thought of putting together a dossier and having the birth mother approve you or not approve you just felt really awful to me and unlikely that we could actually make a good connection." Like Emma, others were worried that they would not be selected by (or make connections with) birth mothers and therefore avoided domestic private adoption altogether.

Women also avoided domestic adoption out of the fear that birth mothers would back out of an arrangement or attempt to reclaim a child placed with them. This situation had actually happened to several women in my study. Eloise Nolan had invested over a year of her time and $10,000 before a birth mother backed out of an arrangement. Jean Kerne found herself even farther along in the process before the birth mother reneged on their agreement: "She was two months pregnant. We connected with her. We followed her through her entire pregnancy, paid her all the money, on and on, went out there. The baby was born; we went out there. We were in the hospital when the baby was born. We took the baby home. And on the eighth day she changed her mind. And that was like—it was like a death. That was so bad."

High-profile cases of surrogates or birth parents attempting to reclaim children (such as "Baby Lenore," "Baby M," and "Baby Richard") solidified these fears. Speaking of how such highly publicized cases propelled her decision to pursue international adoption, Emma Moore stated, "After experiencing a lot of infertility problems, I was just not willing to take that risk." Amanda Holmquist, who had previously adopted domestically, said she did not want to do another state adoption for similar reasons. Even though she had already successfully adopted a white child through the state, she too viewed the likelihood of an interrupted adoption high enough to dissuade her from trying again.

The trend toward open adoptions in the United States, in which all members of the adoption triad (birth parents, adoptive parents, and child) know about and are often involved in the lives of each other, was also viewed as problematic. Open adoptions have led to a more open and fluid concept of family (Modell 1994; Pertman 2000), but the participants in my study were largely unwilling to contemplate creating a family that incorporated interactions with the birth family. At the time they were making their adoption decisions, the parents in my study weren't, as Holly Pritchard put it, "keen on having a lot—having to deal with a biological family." It was a way of "doing family" (Nelson 2006)—of being mothers or fathers—that they found unattractive, at least in their pre-adoption state. They wanted to have an exclusive kinship relationship with their child that was not complicated by the knowledge of or involvement with birth parents or extended birth families. They understood an exclusive kinship to be nearly impossible with a domestic placement. They were drawn to international adoption because of the distance it would provide from birth parents. Adoption agencies know this and stress the forfeiture of parental birth rights as one of the attractive features of international adoption.

Ironically, the distance from birth mothers that participants reported as so attractive during the adoption process was actually mourned by some once their families were established. Priscilla Anderson, who adopted her daughter Kristen from China, said, "The anonymity of the parents—which now I think is not good, I think that is going to be really hard for

Kristen—at the time to me that seemed safer, which I guess was maybe a little selfish."

Priscilla's comment about feeling "safer" in international adoption (versus domestic) is indicative of the general decision to pursue an overseas placement. International adoption was understood to be less risky in terms of expended time and finances, paperwork difficulties, and emotional vulnerability. The fact that most children available for international placements are non-black was important. Also significant was the fact that internationally adopted children are most often legally free for adoption at the time of placement. The distance from birth parents in international adoption—that birth parents do not select adoptive parents, cannot contact them, and are often unknown—was extremely attractive as well. Given this orientation—wanting a young, non-black child who does not come with possibly complicated birth parent interaction— once the decision to adopt was made, the choice to pursue an international placement over a domestic one was a relatively quick one for the majority of women with whom I spoke.[13] The real decision for most was choosing from which country they should adopt.

Choosing Russia, Choosing China

Interviews with parents revealed a spectrum of factors taken into consideration when choosing an adoptive country. Parents are, of course, limited by the countries that have international adoption programs and by those available through U.S. adoption agencies. The list of prospective countries changes as countries close or open their doors to foreign placements. In the early 1990s, when the women who spoke with me were exploring international adoption, China and Russia were emerging as sites for foreign placements.

International adoption programs have requirements for

international-adoptive parents that vary from country to country. Just as parents use particular criteria to select a particular kind of child, government programs use criteria to encourage the formation of particular kinds of families. In some countries, older (or younger), divorced, recently married, homosexual, overweight, mentally ill, and disabled prospective parents are prohibited from adopting.

Restrictions regarding age and marital status in many adoptive countries in the 1990s steered people toward Russia or China. These restrictions vary by country and agency and also change over time. For example, in 2001, the Chinese government began actively to restrict the international adoption of Chinese children by lesbians. Social workers completing home studies for applicants who were living with an adult person of the same sex had to prepare reports attesting that the applicants were not homosexual. In May 2007, China instituted even tighter restrictions and outlawed single-parent adoptions, effectively shutting down China as a site for adoption for lesbians. Others restricted from adopting from China in 2007 included people taking medications for depression and those with a BMI (body mass index) equal to or greater than forty.

But during the time period the parents I spoke with adopted, both China and Russia had relatively lenient policies regarding lesbian, single, divorced, and older parents compared to other popular countries for international adoption. As Rachel Abramson joked, she and her husband "were already too old for a lot of the countries that wanted younger parents, and China either in their wisdom or their craziness likes older parents." (As detailed earlier, Kay Johnson and colleagues have argued that the age minimum of thirty-five in China to adopt was put in place to limit domestic adoption by Chinese citizens, not to encourage international adoption by older parents.) These more flexible policies were one of the main reasons participants chose China or Russia from which to adopt their children. Other popular adoption programs at the time, such as Korea or Colombia, had tighter restrictions regarding the age and marital status of adopters.

The age of children available in particular countries also shaped the choice of adoptive country. Participants in the study overwhelmingly had a strong preference to adopt as young a child as possible, which is typical of contemporary U.S. adoptive parents (Melosh 2002; Zelizer 1985). While the procedures and logistics of international adoptions preclude the adoption of newborns (which is possible in private domestic adoption), in the 1990s both China and Russia were countries in which older, divorced, or remarried couples could adopt infants. The women in my study adopted children from the age of five months to three years, with an average age of sixteen months.[14] As with Lorraine Burg, who adopted her daughter from China at five months, participants wanted infants in order to "experience as much of childhood" as they could. Like Esther Levenson, who adopted her son from Russia when he was seventeen months old, mothers also "did not want to go for a child that had been institutionalized for too long." Participants were fearful of the effects that institutionalization has been reported to have on development and attachment (see Sloutsky 1997). With Korean or Colombian adoptions, stricter policies would have meant that the majority of women in my study would have only been able to adopt older children. Age restrictions, therefore, strongly influenced the parental choice of China or Russia over other countries for international adoption.

Another factor taken into consideration by parents was the length of the adoption process, including time spent abroad. This varies widely from country to country. As detailed above, at the time these parents adopted, both China and Russia required only one trip to the country and both had relatively quick paperwork processing and adoption procedure times. This contrasted with other countries that required multiple trips or extended stays in-country.

The logistics and practicalities regarding age and marital restrictions, costs, length of adoption process, and the age of available children were relatively similar for both China and Russia in the 1990s when the women who spoke with me adopted their children, especially when compared to other programs. In presenting their adoption narratives, many parents framed their decision of China or Russia as a comparative one between these two countries. Racial preferences modified by health concerns constituted the main factor that mothers articulated to describe their decision between the two.

The desire for white infants propelled many to Russia. Parents reported wanting children who were similar to them in phenotype, who would look "as if begotten" (Modell 1994). This privileging of whiteness in their decision was closely aligned with (and often expressed as) a strong emphasis on cultural proximity between parent and child. Women whose families contained a variety of European ethnicities explained the similarity between their own cultural foods, holidays, and traditions and those of Russia. These similarities were seen as a natural conduit through which understanding and transmitting of Russian culture could be integrated into the family easily. They assumed little change would actually have to take place within the family in order to fulfill the understood responsibility of culture keeping. These mothers felt a connection to Russia through their own ethnic heritage. Like many Russia-adoptive mothers, Theresa Fischer had a desire to "share a northern European heritage." Esther Levenson and her husband chose to go to Russia because "we both had Eastern European blood in us and we wanted to make as much of a match as we could," both "culturally and physically."

The parents who adopted from Russia hoped that a monoracial and ethnically similar adoption would ease the transition into a family and allow for a sharing of racial similarity to buffer against the stigma of nonbiological kinship made obvious by differences in phenotype between parents and child. For these parents, adopting a white child meant the ability to avoid the problems they understood to arise from cross-racial placements: prejudice, racism, stigma, and identity issues. As Emma Moore said, "I did think if we adopted from Russia it's probably likely that the child would be Caucasian and that would be one less thing to deal with."

Many families explicitly did not want a child of color. It was not only a desire for whiteness, therefore, but a rejection of nonwhiteness that made Russia and Eastern Europe popular sources for children. One of the mothers, Jean Kerne, reflected that "we didn't want a darker skin or a Chinese . . . to be honest, we just felt we weren't comfortable with that." White children, they expressed, could also be more easily integrated into a white family. They wanted their children to "blend in" physically with their families and communities. Adopting a white child meant that parents and extended family did not have to extend beyond their racial comfort zone. These participants saw monoracial adoption within white families as a way in which race and racial issues could be avoided. Parents with this perspective felt that dealing with issues of nonbiological kinship and adoption would be enough for them and their children to deal with and that the additional issue of race was best avoided. These parents chose Russia because the majority of children available are classified as white in the United States' racial schema.

These parents also saw whiteness as a shared identity that would facilitate bonding between parent and child. For example, when asked why she adopted from Russia, Myra Stockdale emphasized whiteness as a cultural identity she could share with her child, feeling that "the assimilation process would be easier both for the child and for myself" since being white is "my background, my history, and my culture." She stated emphatically, "You know, I'm white. That's who I am. So that's why [I adopted from Russia]." Whiteness not only protected families from stigma, women argued, but was an identity through which bonds could be established and nurtured with their children. In other words, mothers reported a desire for a deep kinship connection they assumed could be forged through sharing whiteness with a child.

The women who adopted from China also considered race and culture when making their adoption decisions. They also desired a deep kinship connection with their children. They did not assume, however, unlike those parents who adopted from Russia, that shared whiteness was a necessary part of that equation. They did not seek to create a family that racially resembled one "as if begotten" (Modell 1994). Instead, almost all of them went outside their own ethnic and racial heritage when choosing a birth country (one participate had a partial Chinese ethnic heritage). They were, however, also displaying clear racial preferences. As noted earlier, although these women felt comfortable adopting interracially, they did not want to adopt black children. Others scholars have noted that the decision to adopt from China is often made in relation to a racial hierarchy where Asian-ness is favored because it is seen as closer to whiteness than to blackness (Dorow 2006b; Rothman 2005).

The decisions to adopt from China, however, involved not only an avoidance of black children. Asian adoptions by whites are often characterized as a fashion trend in the popular press, with Chinese daughters characterized as the latest "must-have" accessory. While this was not corroborated by my research, there were women in my study with children from China who reported being drawn to Asian children specifically because they were "cute and special." These women reported a strong attraction to Chinese people—especially infants or children—that cannot simply be seen as a rejection of blackness and a desire for "near-whiteness." This can be seen in Shirley McIntosh's comments: "I always wanted a Chinese baby. They're special and amazing. I always tell [my daughter], the best kids come from China. Whenever she sees a Chinese baby she says, 'Look Ma, a Chinese baby, your favorite!' "

This objectification by adoptive mothers of Asian girls focused specifically on racialized features and, in that way, bordered on Asian fetish. When Rachel Abramson spoke about her daughters' "Chinese-ness," for example, she focused on how beautiful she found their bodies: "I just love my daughters' Chinese-ness. I just love their hair and their eyes. I just love everything about them and talk about how beautiful and wonderful they are all the time."

Other mothers were excited about the idea of embarking on an education into Chinese culture. Nancy Thorne's sentiments echoed those of many participants when she stated, "I thought China was a culture I would feel comfortable with sharing, you know, learning about with my daughter and understanding more about." Like Nancy, others understood culture keeping to be a necessary component of international-adoptive mothering and sought China as a country that, culturally, was interesting and exciting to them. Some women had been contemplating China adoption for years, before international adoption was even a possibility, because they were interested in China and wanted to engage with the culture in a meaningful way. Likewise, several women felt strong personal connections to China, cultivated through time spent in China, language or cultural study, or feelings of cultural affinity, although not through their own ethnic heritage.

In reconstructing their adoption decisions for me, the China-adoptive mothers did not problematize the interracial aspect of their families. For some, interraciality was even desired precisely because they believed an interracial placement would make it apparent that the family was formed through adoption. When I asked Charlotte Gordon why she found this to be important, she replied, "I didn't want it to feel to the child as although it was something to be ashamed of or to be a secret. And I just felt like it would be a little bit easier to be out there to start. It [*sic*] wouldn't have to say, 'Oh excuse me, guess what? Did you know I was adopted?' "

Rather than a desire to have their children "blend in," some China-adoptive mothers wanted the fact of adoption to be obvious to everyone because they felt this would be emotionally and psychologically more healthy for their children. These women understood the cross-racial aspect of their families as a way of making nonbiological kinship clear to everyone, which would honor adoption as a valid and even preferred way of forming families. They saw potential problems—such as nondisclosure about adoption and mistaken biological connectedness, that could result in psychological trauma for the child—arising when nonbiological kinship is hidden due to racial similarities between parents and child.

A much smaller factor reported in the decision to pursue Chinese over Russian adoption (and vice versa) was gender preference. Some parents who adopted from China were drawn to that country by the fact that the overwhelming majority of children available for adoption are girls.[15] Several women who chose China had specific political concerns regarding the gender discrimination faced by infant girls in China. For these mothers, feminist principles guided their selection of China. There are also parents who desire boys, such as several in my study, and who therefore avoid China and pursue Russian adoptions.[16]

The overwhelming factor, however, that most women spoke of when discussing their decision to adopt from China (over Russia) was their desire for a non-black *healthy* infant. Priscilla Anderson's comments were indicative of this focus: "We just said China, great, without having any history with the country or anything. But it is just that we wanted a healthy baby. That was completely the motivation." China-adoptive parents reported that Chinese children were the most healthy available internationally. This idea is widely touted by adoption agencies that specialize in China adoption. Agencies regularly advertise the health of the babies as a unique feature of their Chinese programs. They argue, as do China-adoptive parents, that Chinese adoptees are more likely to be healthy due to the unique factors that shape child abandonment in China. Nancy Thorne shared this theory with me: "Typically, the babies coming out of China are healthy. Healthier than a lot of other countries. The Chinese give up their children, surrender their children, for cultural reasons. Typically it is, it's for the one-child, male, inheritance piece and so I sort of felt that the women were probably taking better care of themselves because they didn't know until they delivered. It wasn't from poverty, which it is in a lot of other countries where the mother—birth mothers—may not have taken as good care of themselves."

Stories of health problems of children adopted out of Eastern Europe (Romania and Russia, in particular) were prevalent in the press in the early 1990s when many of the participants in my study adopted. High rates of alcoholism in the Russian population, signaling high risk of in utero alcohol exposure, drew significant attention. Socio-emotional problems influencing attachment and bonding were also frequently reported. Women who adopted from China had heard these stories, and they were among the reasons the women avoided Russia and turned toward China. Priscilla Anderson explained how the news reports affected her decision-making: "I have heard scary things about Russian kids and their attachment problems. And the Chinese babies from what I heard are healthy and well loved at the time that they were put into the system."

Mothers who adopted from Russia had heard these stories

as well with some referencing them when discussing a stigma they felt their children faced. Further complicating matters was the fact that medical reports on Russian orphans often included diagnoses difficult for Westerners to interpret. Dr. Jane Aronson ("The Orphan Doctor") argues on her website *orphandoctor.com* that "physicians in Russia have a unique perspective of the health of newborn infants. This is the system of 'defectology' wherein infants are considered inherently defective and then over time, their 'defects' resolve." Because of this, it has been argued that incorrect health diagnoses can be found in children's medical records (see Cox 1991). On her website, Aronson lists conditions regularly found on Russia adoptees' medical reports. These include "neuro-reflex-hyper-excitability syndrome (a description of a high strung infant) . . . hypertensive-hydrocephalic syndrome (increased pressure and increased amount of cerebrospinal fluid in the ventricles of the brain) . . . and intestinal dysbacteriosis (bacteria or normal flora of the intestines)." Russia-adoptive parents report, and adoption medical specialists confirm, that these (and other) diagnoses given to children in Russia are often not corroborated once the children are adopted.[17]

Russia-adoptive parents reported that their adoption agencies explained to them from the beginning of the adoption process that they would probably find some disconcerting information on the medical reports they received. Some parents were told that Russians deliberately falsified medical reports in order for children to be made available for international adoption. Dotty Cohen reflected, "They kind of prepared us that this is what's going to be. Sure enough, I remember getting medical data on my older daughter. Had you read it and really interpreted it well, you would have thought that she was extremely brain-damaged. I mean, it was the diagnosis."

Despite the fact that participants had been warned about unique Russian health diagnoses, receiving a referral for a particular child that included serious health conditions was disconcerting. Coupled with the popular image in the press of the medically and psychologically unhealthy Russian adoptee, this scared many women.

Adoption agencies have attempted to temper this fear. For instance, Children's Hope International tells prospective adoptive parents in their information guide, "For an orphan growing up in an institution, physical and emotional development can be at a slower rate. But once in the embrace of a loving family the child in most cases will quickly catch up to her peers" (n.d.). Most adoption agencies make this argument in their pre-adoptive guides—that a nurturing, loving home will reverse most health and behavioral issues adoptees may present. One agency directly states, "It is a myth that most Russian children offered for adoption have FAS [fetal alcohol syndrome] or FAE [fetal alcohol exposure]" (Christian World Adoption 2007).

Despite these messages of "love conquers all," the Russia-adoptive mothers in my study still had concerns regarding the health of children referred to them. They managed these concerns in several ways. Some participants insisted on receiving videos in order to assess the children's development and physiques (for example, to check for physical markers of fetal alcohol syndrome). Some prospective mothers consulted adoption specialists—health care professionals who focus on the assessment of children pre-adoption and the care of children post-adoption. At the time, this industry was just emerging and many prospective mothers did not have access to such services; those who could not locate specialists (or didn't try because they did not know such specialists existed) relied upon their own physicians or friends employed in the health care profession to assess the children, from videos or medical reports. Other participants insisted that referred children be seen at clinics with American medical personnel, with the reports then sent to them for evaluation. Others had Russian-speaking friends or acquaintances call orphanage directors in order to obtain more detailed health information.

Many agencies today encourage parents to make use of these medical and developmental evaluation mechanisms. Some agencies today even provide some of these services as part of their adoption "packages." When the families in my study adopted, however, most needed to request or secure these additional evaluations on their own. Although quite common today, videos were not regularly given to prospective adopters in the early to mid-1990s and people sometimes had to change agencies in order to receive one.

Several women rejected referred children upon receiving more detailed information or upon the recommendation of health care professionals. Most, however, received additional health information that was positive, countering previous reports. They also found reassurance in seeing previously adopted Russian children who were healthy and thriving with their new parents. These measures allowed people to move forward with their Russian adoptions despite their fears.

The China-adoptive mothers in my study had also received scant medical information. Some had also requested additional health evaluations, but this was not a dominant theme in their narratives. Concerns about SARS and lead poisoning among Chinese adoptees were not yet issues of concern for China-adoptive parents. Rather, the choice of China as an adoptive country itself was *the* significant measure participants in my study used to address concerns about health.

It is important to note that some China- and Russia-adoptive families did experience health and developmental issues with their children post-adoption. These ranged from infections or disabilities known at the time of adoption to cognitive or behavioral issues that had not been noticed or had not yet emerged when the children were brought into the United

States (such as ADD/ADHD or Sensory Integration Disorder). The medical literature on the post-adoption status of international adoptees points to health issues and developmental delays found among both Chinese and Russian adopted children, although differences have been noted. For example, in their study of 123 infants and toddlers adopted from China, East Asia, and Russia, Pomerleau and colleagues found craniofacial abnormalities and eczema more prevalent in the Chinese group and gastrointestinal infections and "neurological signs more frequent in the Russian group" (2005, 450). Important factors for health issues and delays emphasized in the literature focus on the length of time children spend in institutionalized care and the intensity of pre-adoptive deprivation associated with countries of origin (Meese 2005).

Both China- and Russia-adoptive mothers managed any remaining health uncertainty by placing it within a larger rubric of uncertainty in parenting in general. All parenting, they argued—both adoptive and biological parenting—entails unknown challenges, including health concerns, and one must be prepared to deal with them if one wants to parent. Russia-adoptive mother Cheryl Haley contextualized health concerns in adoption by speaking of problems "popping up" in children, regardless of adoptive status, saying, "It's like, with any child, really, I mean, you could have your own biological child and certainly have a problem. Things happen at birth, cerebral palsy or something . . . Keep in mind that anyone can have a medical problem. Anything can come up in the future."

Cheryl's argument was shared by many adoptive parents—both those who adopted from Russia and those from China. In many interviews, paralleling the experiences of adoptive and biological parents and seeing them both as a "leap of faith" were common. Russia-adoptive mother Emma Moore expressed sentiments similar to Cheryl's: "You just take a leap of faith and hope that everything will work out. This is true if they are biological. They often have challenges with their children that we don't perceive."

Adoption as a "leap of faith" is quite poignant in light of the scant historical and health information on prospective children given to all international-adoptive parents and the misinformation allegedly given to parents with children from Russia. It is also emblematic of how women with children from China spoke about their formation of interracial families. Most of the people who spoke with me argued that their choice to adopt internationally from China and Russia came down to this: a leap into the unknown that just "felt right." They spoke of their choices as "natural," ones that "clicked" and "made sense" within their families. Vivian Lutz expressed this when she stated, "There was just so much that just felt really good and right about adopting from China and it just seemed to make sense given who we were and what we wanted to do."

Conclusion

Many adoptive parents rely upon the idea of fate or religious intervention to understand and describe how they ended up adopting from China or Russia and how they were matched with a particular child (i.e., "matches made in heaven"). The China-adoptive community, for example, has adapted the Chinese legend of the red thread (one traditional version has a thread connecting destined lovers) to read specifically about and narrate the international adoption experience, with the thread now connecting newborn Chinese infants with their destined international-adoptive parents.[18]

As this chapter reveals, however, adopting internationally is not a situation in which people suddenly wake up one day and find themselves. Becoming an international adoptive mother is a deliberate process. Women who adopt their chil-

dren internationally cannot "accidentally" fall into parenthood. There is too much work involved in family formation:
too many decisions to be made, too much paperwork to fill out
and file, and too much money changing hands. When mothers reconstructed their adoption stories for me, it became
clear that their adoption decision-making trajectories were directed by the desire to make the process of becoming and being a family—a particular kind of family—easier. The women
wanted families who were accepted in their communities.
They wanted healthy children with whom they could bond.
They wanted a deep exclusive parent/child kinship with their
children. In order to fulfill this desire for a particular kind of
family, they avoided the birth parent conundrum of domestic
adoption and the adoption of black children.

The decision to adopt internationally, and the choice of
adoptive country, is made in the context of dominant ideologies of race, ethnicity, and the family. Both Russia- and China-
adoptive mothers who spoke with me wanted healthy, young,
non-black children. This desire was the filter through which
their adoption decisions were made. Both China- and Russia-
adoptive mothers relied, therefore, upon notions of race and
the family, but to different effects. Russia-adoptive mothers
wanted to replicate a biological family by avoiding racial difference. They did so to seek acceptance of their family and to
facilitate bonding. They made connections between their ethnic heritages and Russia, and framed Russia adoption as a logical choice. Likewise, China-adoptive mothers characterized
China as the logical choice for their families. They sought acceptance for their families through the avoidance of adopting
black children and through privileging "Asian-ness." They too
desired acceptance of their families. Some reported contemplating Russia adoption because of this desire but did not feel
they could risk the potential health problems they understood

to characterize Russian adoptees. Some Russia adopters stated that having successfully completed a Russia adoption, they felt they could "now do China."

The decisions to adopt from either China or Russia are both framed by potential dilemmas women saw emerging from nonbiological kinship. In the choice of adoptive country, they managed those dilemmas differently, but both sets of women made their decisions in relation to ideologies of race and kinship. The primary arena in which these potential problems were negotiated once their children "came home" was in culture keeping.

3

The Culture Keeping Agenda

You have to make an effort to bring culture into your
home, into your family. You have to want to do that.
You have to want to be interested in doing that.
It can't be a burden. You have to want to do it.
　—Stacey Dita, China-adoptive mother

It's important that she know what her roots are,
because at some point she will ask. She will
need to know and I can tell her.
　—Christina Denison, Russia-adoptive mother

Engagement with a foreign culture is promoted by the adoption industry as one of the attractive features of international adoption. Adoption agencies use representations of culture as a medium through which adoption programs are marketed to prospective adopters. Programs are introduced in adoption materials through visual representations of historic landmarks (the Great Wall of China, for example, and, for Russia, St. Basil's Cathedral in Red Square). These images immediately signal historic "China" or "Russia" to and for Western eyes.

Agencies also market the ethnic (yet ethnically malleable) child. Pictures of children in adoption materials show them post-adoption, happy in the arms of their new parents. They are presented as familial, in a white, middle-class, U.S. context, yet with an interesting splash of foreign ethnic color. They are often shown in ethnic garb, especially if they are Asian, although Eastern European children are also sometimes presented this way. The ethnic clothing of the children, however, is typically the fancy "traditional" dress sold to adoptive parents, not the clothing that is worn daily by children (especially those in state care) in their birth countries. In these first images many adoptive parents receive of an international adoption program, the children themselves are offered as innately and desirably (and manageably) ethnic.

These glossy images are displayed by adoption agencies in visually appealing concert with statements about the importance of "embracing" the adopted child's birth culture. During an information session for prospective clients, for example, one showed a marketing video that contained beautiful montages of breathtakingly beautiful historic sites in Russia and cherubic, towheaded, post-adopted children. Following the video, the adoption agency director looked out at the group and emphatically stated, "You are not only adopting a child, you are adopting a culture. You need to know that." This framing of culture as attractive, necessary, and innate to the child is the professionally prescribed position of the adoption industry. It is also a marketing strategy and can be seen to appeal to the cultural longings of a largely white, middle-class clientele.

How do mothers interpret this idea of culture and the edict that they must engage in it? How do they understand their own motivations to keep culture? What ideologies of children, mothering, and ethnicity do they embrace and activate in articulating their decision to socialize their children along ethnic lines? This chapter examines these questions by focusing on the articulated motivations of Russia- and China-adoptive mothers who actively engage in culture keeping with their children.

Variations in Motivations

Adoption agencies tell parents they should embrace their children's birth culture and point them in the direction of what "culture" means, yet most do not give parents detailed guidelines on how to keep culture in meaningful ways beyond the acknowledgment of cultural difference through participation in agency-sponsored "culture days." Moreover, particular ideologies of children, mothering, and ethnicity are activated in interpretations of culture keeping. These ideologies position mothers differently depending upon the racial composition of their families. Agencies and the adoption community encourage a variety of understandings of children's particular ethnic identities and "cultural needs" depending upon the country of birth. There is a good deal of room, therefore, for variation in culture keeping perspectives and practices. As this chapter explores, these variations are displayed in how messages of culture keeping are broadcast, how adoptive parents interpret those messages, and the ideologies mothers call upon to make sense of their cultural engagement.

The variations in ideologies used to support culture keeping engagement are strikingly noticeable when comparing the motivations of China- and Russia-adoptive families. The major distinction between China- and Russia-adoptive families first appears to be one of personal preference. Mothers with children from China appear, as a group, more interested in connecting their children to birth culture than do mothers with children from Russia. Culture keeping was more common among China-adoptive families than Russia-adoptive ones. However, when examined more closely, it becomes evident that more is involved in culture keeping than personal preference.

While the adoption industry markets culture for *all* international adoption programs, they facilitate culture keeping more intensely in some programs than others. For example, the cultural education of adopters is integrated into the adoption process for China adopters much more so than it is for those with children from Russia. China-adoptive parents are scheduled for guided tours of famous cultural landmarks during their trips in-country to collect their children, while organized sightseeing is not an institutionalized part of Russia-adoption. China adopters even receive a mandate to keep culture directly from the Chinese government (Rojewski and Rojewski 2001), while those adopting from Russia experience no such instruction. Although China-adoptive mothers reported that, while in China, they were often too emotionally and physically overwhelmed by becoming new parents to actually absorb much in the way of a cultural education, the message was clearly articulated to them that they were expected to learn about China and impart cultural information to their children. In these ways, China adopters receive more direct encouragement in the adoption process than do Russia adopters to keep culture.

A simple explanation seems plausible for this difference in parental interest and institutionalized encouragement: China-adoptive mothers are (usually) parenting racial/ethnic minority children and Russia-adoptive mothers (usually) are not. As this chapter argues, how adoptive mothers (and the adoption industry) think about race and the needs of their children depending upon their racial status *does* profoundly shape how culture keeping is encouraged, perceived, and enacted.

This difference brings to light the ways phenotype, cultural identification, and cultural engagement are understood to be inextricably intertwined (see Tuan 1998). The darker the child, this view of ethnicity holds, the deeper the need to keep culture; the lighter the child, the less resonance culture has in their lives. This mirrors the popular idea that people of color innately have more authentic and richer ethnic lives than do whites (see hooks 1992). According to this perspective, adoptive mothers with racial minority children should keep culture in order to replicate the ethnic experiences their child would have had if they had remained with their birth family.

But if this framing was consistently held in the adoption community, only those families with children of color would engage in culture keeping. As my research makes evident, this is not the case. Rather, perspectives and practices of culture keeping vary. Among both China- and Russia-adoptive mothers in my sample, there were intense culture keepers and those who did little to connect their children to their ethnic heritages. While culture keeping is much more prevalent among China adopters, this range can be found among both groups. Later chapters look at why some mothers, particularly those with children from Russia, are resistant to the incorporation of ethnic practices into their families' lives. This chapter focuses on the articulated motivations of those mothers who do keep culture.

The Familial Context

To begin a discussion of culture keeping motivations, it is important to understand why these cultural practices are framed as familial activities. After all, ethnicity is not constructed, nor does it occur, exclusively within the family. Parents and family members do, however, play a central role in shaping the ethnic experiences and practices of their young children. As Karen Hansen remarks, "Ultimately, parents are primarily responsible for their children—legally and culturally. They have some agency in the choices they make about raising their children" (2001, 40). Part of the agency parents are able to express in raising their children is in socialization—in the development of specific identities they choose to cultivate for their children. Parent-directed child socialization is especially true for contemporary middle-class children who have little self-directed free time and whose parents invest large amounts of time and money into cultivating their identities (Lareau 2003).

Families are understood to be the primary site of childhood identity formation. Families are (most often) the first group through which children learn about the world around them and their place in it. Identities are thought to be actually ascribed through families: children are understood to be Nigerian or Catholic or working-class because they come from Nigerian, Catholic, or working-class families. In a volume on family ethnicity, for example, Harriette Pipes McAdoo writes, "When we examine ourselves, we find that who we are and who we can become depends in great part on who we started out to be. This is found within our families. Our ethnicity cannot be separated from our families" (1999, 3).

But what of children who are separated from their natal families—children who traverse between families, ethnicities, cultures, and nations? What about children who are attached to one family at birth and then transferred to an institution and then, perhaps, to another family still? What of their "family ethnicity"? By examining these children whose histories have traversed more than one culture and nation and family, we can see the process through which social identities are constructed, rather than thinking of them in terms of primordial origins.

The construction of social identities, even those that are popularly seen as ascribed at birth, such as gender, require effort and labor. Although we are (most often, but not always) born male or female, it takes work to become a girl or boy, as feminist scholarship has shown (see Lorber 1995; West and Zimmerman 1987). For young children this is especially noticeable. Blue or pink clothes are put on, gender-specific names are selected, and gender-appropriate toys are bought and played with. For young children, these gendering activities are largely performed for them and to them by others. A newborn has little concern whether a hair bow will properly convey "girl" to her adoring public. Yet it matters to the adults in her life who labored to get the bow into place. And it matters to strangers who gaze into her stroller, understand she is indeed a girl, and, because of the way understandings of gender shape interaction, thus know how to interact with her caregivers about her.

We can see that these gendering activities matter when there is some ambiguity about sex status or when strangers misidentify a girl as a boy (Lucal 2008). Strangers are to "read" children's gender markers properly, and parents and adult caregivers are to convey them properly. This doesn't always happen, of course. People do resist and subvert hegemonic masculinity or femininity. Nor is adult behavior that socializes children always consciously intended, always mainstream, and never without constraint, conflict, or contradictory feelings. Ideas about the proper display of masculinity and femininity vary across history as well. Regardless of the content or methods through which masculinity or femininity is accomplished (or resisted), it is done so in interaction with others and not simply as an articulation of primordial identity—even if that is how it is understood by those performing that work (West and Zimmerman 2002). For children, especially very young children, interactional gender work is done by adults (parents, caregivers, and others) to, with, and for the child.

Children, of course, have agency; they are actors in their own lives. Children do, to the great chagrin of many parents, resist or subvert parental socialization efforts (think of the pink-clad princess-obsessed daughters of feminist parents). But the socialization of children—especially young children—is largely directed and controlled by adults who work to construct specific positions for their children in the world. Sometimes this work is deliberate and conscious, such as when hegemonic femininity or masculinity is challenged, other times it is simply "going with the flow" and allowing prescribed dominant ideas about gender to shape parent/child interaction. All of this labor, however, occurs in the presence of others (or with others in mind) for whom those displays have meaning. This type of labor occurs not only in extreme examples (such as in child beauty pageants) but is rather an ongoing, daily, continual process (Lorber 1995).

Like gender, ethnic identity is similarly constructed. It is not innate, static, or fixed, although, like gender, it is often popularly thought to be. Ethnic identities are constructed for children using the "material" of culture. However, culture itself is not fixed; it is not "a shopping cart that comes to us already loaded with a set of historical cultural goods. Rather we construct culture by picking and choosing items from the shelves of the past and present" (Nagel 1994, 162). In other words, we collectively construct ethnicity by using certain items and practices we have defined as cultural. And like gender, for young children "the picking and choosing" of cultural items and practices is completed and transmitted largely through the work of adults—especially female caregivers (di Leonardo 1987; Stack and Burton 1993; Glenn 1986).

Although culture transmission is symbolically and often empirically the purview of mothers, not all mothers experience the labor of childhood ethnic socialization equally. How mothers think about the identities of their families directs the kinds of ethnic practices they structure for their children. But such practiced ethnicity is not merely the outcome of individual belief or effort, but also a product of how others think about and react to families. The very options for ethnic identity made available to children (directed by their caregivers) are shaped and constrained by others outside their immediate families (Nagel 1994). In other words, ethnic "self concept" is "to some extent asserted and to some extent imposed or assigned" (Cornell 1988, 27). The social context of individual lives—including racial, ethnic, and social class locations—can facilitate, encourage, constrain, or even require certain types of ethnic socialization.

Race and the Ethnic Socialization of Children

Racial status and racial meanings inform cultural engagement in important ways in the United States (Berbrier 2007). The expression of ethnic identity, shaped by race, has varying consequences for different populations in the United States.[1] This is particularly salient when contrasting the experiences of white women and women of color as they engage in the ethnic socialization of their children.

Engagement with culture among mothers of color is often thought of as "bicultural" in that they must prepare their children to negotiate "two worlds": that of their own racial/ethnic group and dominant white mainstream society (Carothers 1998). Given the complexity and plurality of contemporary U.S. society and the construction of multiple social identities, it is problematic to paint racial ethnic culture and white culture as monolithic polar opposites (Kibria 1997). At the same time, however, it is important to acknowledge that part of the cultural education of children of color engaged in by their mothers is preparing them to deal with an institutional and interpersonal racism that white children largely avoid. As Patricia Hill Collins notes, "For women of color, the subjective experience of mothering/motherhood is inextricably linked to the sociocultural concern on racial ethnic communities—one does not exist without the other" (1994, 47).

The literature on African American mothering points to the importance of race socialization that occurs in the family context (Banks-Wallace and Parks 2001; Collins 1990; Kibria 2002a). Suzanne Carothers, for example, observed black women using "dramatic enactments" in which mothers deliberately placed their children in situations to witness interactions between blacks and whites in order to teach their children how to deal with racism. Carothers notes, "It is important for mothers to teach their daughters how to cope with the world; therefore, they do not hide the world from them" (1998, 323–24).

Many do, however, also seek to protect their children from the pain of racism (Banks-Wallace and Parks 2001; Collins 1991). Studies point to the strategy used by African American mothers of attempting to ensure their children's safety through numbers. In her 2003 study on social class differences in child-rearing, Annette Lareau noted that middle-class black mothers require their children's extracurricular activities involve other black children (if only a few—the real concern was that their children were not the *only* black child).

Women of color also try and construct racially safe environments for their children through their engagement in cultural communities. Some do so through creating ethnically informed environments for their children. JoAnne Banks-Wallace and Lennette Parks noted African American women deliberately purchasing ethnic goods (artwork, books, and toys) in order to create "aesthetically pleasing environments" that reflect the children's heritage in positive ways (2001); in doing so, women of color attempt to "foster a meaningful racial identity in children within a society that denigrates people of color" (Collins 1994, 57). Lynet Uttal reported African American and Latina women attempting to find day care for their young children within their own racial ethnic communities with the hopes of ensuring that their children are both protected from racism and exposed to particular cultural practices and values (1998). Likewise, Nazli Kibria found among her second-generation Chinese American and Korean American informants a "sense of ethnic consciousness and pride" instilled through "their families' community embeddedness and active efforts to educate the young into Chinese or Korean culture" (2002a, 46).

These studies point to deliberate strategies, including ethnic socialization, used by mothers of color to mitigate racism in the lives of their children. Patricia Hill Collins conceptualizes this as "motherwork," arguing that African American women engage in this labor on behalf of all children in their racial-ethnic community, not only their own (1994). They transmit cultural information to their children not only because of the enjoyment that particular traditions hold and the connection they facilitate to family and ethnic communities, but out of the hope that doing so will help them safely navigate their lives as people of color in a racially stratified society. In this way, ethnic socialization is a reaction to ascribed racial identities and to racism.

In contrast, white mothers of biological white children in the United States enjoy a large degree of flexibility in terms of the content and tenor of the ethnic practices they construct for their families. Without concern for racial safety, they can both choose whether or not to assert an ethnic identity and, due to high levels of intermarriage among whites, they can select from among the available "white" ethnicities within their family history (Waters 1990). As they have considerable distance from the customs, language, and traditions of their ancestors, they can choose which "ethnic" characteristics to enjoy and can easily slip on and off an ethnic identity (or identities) in their day-to-day lives (on St. Patrick's Day, for instance, they can be "100 percent Irish," yet on March 18th they can be nothing but "American" through and through).

Despite the large degree of flexibility and freedom that characterizes white ethnicity, white ethnics understand their ethnicity to be stable and fixed and passed down through family bloodlines (Waters 1990). They attach deep meaning to their ethnic practices and see them as ways to express an inherent piece of their identity and birthright.

Contemporary white ethnic practices are rooted in the

white ethnic revival of the 1960s and 1970s that was characterized by new levels of interest and pride in ethnic roots. Partially in response to the civil rights movement and the increasing emphasis on racial pride among Blacks and Asians, white ethnics sought to distance themselves from "whiteness" and instead emphasize their own historic ethnic oppression (di Leonardo 1984; Jacobson 1998; Waters 1990). Ethnic fairs, ethnic foods, music and books, especially those that romanticized the white "immigrant saga," all became popular among third- and fourth-generation white ethnics attempting to learn about their particular family history and enjoy the culture of their ancestors.

Many whites enjoy symbolic ethnic practices because they understand American whiteness to be bland and one-dimensional—to be lacking an actual "culture" (Drzewiecka and Wong 1999; Waters 1990). Asserting an ethnic identity adds spice to their lives. At the same time it gives them a largely imaginary community of other co-ethnics with whom to identify. Mary Waters writes that for white ethnics, symbolic ethnicity "is the best of all worlds: they can claim to be unique and special while simultaneously finding the community and conformity with others that they crave" (1990, 151).

Culture keeping is encouraged by the adoption industry in a way that taps into this desire for interesting cultural engagement and community. Above all, culture keeping, for mothers who engage in it, is largely pleasurable. For China-adoptive mothers, this pleasure is found not only in the actual "doing" of culture, but in the exploration and consumption of an ethnic minority culture. They display pride in becoming culturally facile with an "exotic" culture. In this we can see, as bell hooks writes, that "ethnicity becomes spice, seasoning that can liven up the dull dish that is mainstream white culture" (1992, 21). Race scholars, such as hooks, conceptualize this type of desire by whites to seek pleasure in the racialized "Other" as inherently problematic.

China-adoptive mothers reported a definite shift in how they thought about and engaged in culture once they adopted their children. Many characterized this shift as propelling them into the "uncharted territory" of engaging with a foreign culture in ways that were not purely symbolic. Although they may have had experience with Irish or Italian symbolic ethnicity, they knew little about integrating Chinese culture into their families' day-to-day lives. Yet they were told by their agencies and the larger adoption community that they should engage their children with their birth culture. They did not question that an authentic Chinese culture existed; they just did not know what exactly it was or how to capture it on their own. Nor were they confident as to the best route for integrating that culture into their families' lives. But they were eager and excited to embark into this "new territory." Adopting internationally gave them license to deeply and publicly do so. As they were among the first wave of Chinese-adopters in the United States, they referred to themselves as "pioneers," as "parents without a road map."

Russia-adoptive mothers also characterized themselves as "pioneers"; however this largely focused on actual travel to Russia rather than new perspectives of culture and race. Figuring out how to integrate Russian-born children into their families' lives was new to them; however, they largely did not report a change or shift in their orientations to cultural engagement. Rather, active Russia-adoptive culture keepers were *already* engaging in white ethnic practices prior to the adoption of their children. These women enjoyed their white ethnic heritages and integrated various aspects of them into their families' lives. The call to keep culture for their adopted children was aligned, therefore, with their more general orientation to cultural practices already established within their families. Mothers simply added Russian cultural practices to the ongoing enjoyment of Scandinavian, Czech, and other ethnic traditions occurring in their households. They found pleasure in expressing their own ethnicity and in adding their new child's cultural practices to their families' repertoire. This confirms Richard Alba's finding that, among white ethnics, "Parents who attach some importance to their ethnic identities are likely to want their children to identify as well" (1990, 205).

In both China- and Russia- adoptive mothers' particular orientations to culture, we can see the impact of 1990s multiculturalism. Culture keeping itself can be seen as an outgrowth of these new ideas about the incorporation and embrace of various cultures and ethnic differences (Anagnost 2000 and 2004; Dorow 2006a; Melosh 2002; Volkman 2003).

While 1970s multiculturalism was focused on "reorganizing education for the benefit of minority students," 1990s multiculturalism emphasized "a recognition, however belated, of the fundamentally multiracial and multiethnic nature of the United States" (Newfield and Gordon 1996, 77). It emphasized a celebration of ethnicity and country of origin and posited cultural education as an important component of promoting "understanding among people of different ethnicities" and building self-esteem in young people (Binder 1999, 229).

The acknowledgment of ethnic difference is framed as especially important for adopted children, who are seen to be at risk for a multitude of disorders (Bartholet 1999; Lifton 1987). "Adopted child syndrome" (a label coined by clinical child psychologist David Kirschner in 1986) includes a wide range of behaviors such as "theft, pathological lying, learning disabilities, setting fires, defiance of authority, preoccupation with excessive fantasy, lack of impulse control, and running away from home" (Carp 1998, 188). These problems, understood to impede bonding with adoptive parents, are thought to be (in part) ameliorated by engagement with culture (Freundlich 2000). Culture keeping, therefore, is framed as a necessary part of ensuring healthy self-esteem in *all* international adoptees, but most especially racial minority children for whom the ethnic gap between themselves and their parents is seen to be widest.

Articulated Motivations for Culture Keeping

The majority of women with children from China who spoke with me framed engagement with birth culture as an important dimension of their mothering responsibilities toward a Chinese child. As Lynn Werden commented, it was "part of creating a healthy individual child." These women anticipated that, by pursuing Chinese cultural activities, talking positively about China, and bringing Chinese-related goods into their home, a love of China and appreciation for things Chinese would translate into a love of self for their child. Comments such as Lorraine Burg's were common: in speaking of her culture keeping motivations, Lorraine reported that one of her main goals was "to offset the negative things that people feel about people from other cultures in this country and to embrace the stuff that makes China unique and makes people proud of being Chinese" in order to give her children "some strength when they have to deal with the negative stuff that people say."

As is reflected in Lorraine's comments, culture keeping was established and is maintained in the China adoption community as an active strategy for families to prepare their children for encounters with racism. Parents hoped to give their children a solid education and appreciation of Chinese culture that would help establish a positive racial identity, thus giving the child a "protective shield" of a sort to rely upon when dealing with racial identity issues. Many mothers framed culture keeping as a way to mitigate the negative impact of race by facilitating self-worth and self-esteem in their children.

In this way, culture keeping can be seen to mirror the practices of many mothers of color in the United States as they seek ethnic pride to counter racism. Racial minority women however, were not seen by the women who spoke with me as mothering role models for learning how to address racial issues for their children. Rather, the mothers in my study conceptualized their "ethnic labor" as distinctly shaped by adoption. They looked, therefore, to the adoption world for lessons, advice, and strategies for negotiating difference.

As noted earlier, the historical debates surrounding domestic transracial adoption and the more recent response regarding race, culture, and family by adult Korean adoptees has had a profound effect on how contemporary adoptive parents think about race and ethnicity. In adoption conference presentations, memoirs (Koh 1981; Robinson 2002; Trenka 2003), collected writings (Cox 1999; Koh 1993; Trenka 2006), films (Liem 2000), and numerous blogs, adult Korean adoptees have highlighted the ways in which isolation from birth culture and forced assimilation into whiteness has been damaging to their own self-esteem and to relations within their families. Seminars and workshops given by adult adoptees are well-attended by adoptive parents hoping to learn the best possible parenting practices and mistakes to avoid with their own children. The "cautionary tales" of Korean adoptees have propelled contemporary adoptive mothers of Asian children to find ways to integrate birth culture into their families' lives (Volkman 2005, 10).

Just as mothers are oriented to engage in culture keeping through the world of adoption, the mechanisms for doing so are largely understood to reside within that world as well. Rather than drawing from their own past experiences or social networks, international-adoptive mothers look to each other and resources in the adoption community in order to learn how to best address racism.

This points to a major difference between women of color and white international-adoptive mothers. Women of color often have access to a cultural education embedded in prior experiences with their families of origin and in their ethnic communities, but this is not always the case. Due to distance from the generation of immigration, "Americanization," or mainstream assimilation efforts, later-generation women of color may have had little in terms of explicit cultural education. Even if they do not pass on ethnic traditions to their children, however, mothers of color have intimate knowledge of navigating race and racism that they can pass onto their children (if they recognize it as such and choose to do so) . This is not the case for the majority of international-adoptive mothers, many of whom report becoming intimately aware of racial and cultural issues *only* through their adoption experiences.

Among my sample, most China-adoptive mothers reported a heightened awareness of racial obligations due to their adoption of Asian children. This is the professionally prescribed position held and disseminated by the adoption industry (i.e., adoption agencies and social workers) and community (i.e., adoptive parents, adoptees, and activists). Most China-adoptive mothers were dedicated to pursuing culture keeping and encouraging self-esteem regarding racial issues in their daughters. They espoused a multicultural or cultural pluralist orientation to race in which ethic origins are honored and racial inequality acknowledged.

Several women in my study were widely read on the topic of race and ethnicity, with a few working professionally in fields that dealt with these issues (as professors, counselors, or psychologists). The majority of China-adoptive mothers thought critically about the ways to address race in their families. They advocated educating their children about race (including differences in phenotype), talking about race and racial issues, and arming them with knowledge to deal with racism. Holly Pritchard spoke of race as a topic that *must* be addressed with international-adoptive families:

> Race is an interesting, complex issue in the United States. I don't purport to be an expert, but the more—I just think communication is really the key, and whatever—lots of parents aren't comfortable talking about it—that's okay, then get the right books, and read the books together, even if you don't use your own words. I think you can get the concepts across. And I think most people, once they've read a couple of those books can start to talk about it with their kids; I mean, in a way it's easier too. It's like dealing with sex when they're a little older; you've got to do it. If you leave it up to everybody else to give them their education, you're making a big mistake.

Holly's views were typical among my participants. Other women (roughly 20 percent of my sample), however, espoused a colorblind orientation to race. Other researchers have noted this variation among adoptive mothers (see Dorow 2006a; Moosenick 2004; Shiao, Tuan, and Rienzi 2004).

Mothers who ascribed to the colorblind perspective did not actively engage in "race talk" with their children. They chose not to "see" race. Shirley McIntosh claimed, "I don't even feel like I'm in an interracial family." Shannon Lynch said that her children "don't have a clue that they're in an interracial family." Similarly, Astrid Tucker claimed not to see her daughter as Chinese:

> When I look at her, she doesn't look Chinese, which sounds very strange. But it used to be we'd be in the supermarket and I'd be pushing her along and people would go, "Oh, she was born in China?" and I'd go, "How can they guess?"

Which was—when you see her, she's obviously Chinese. But to me, she's Natalie. She doesn't look Chinese. She just looks like Natalie. That's how Natalie looks, you know? And I'm always amazed for a second when people say, "Oh, she's from China." "How do you know that?" And then after a second I go, "Okay, that's a stupid question."

Being "blind" to race and racial difference is a popular strategy used in mainstream society (especially by whites) in attempts to mitigate racism. By applying that model to their children, these mothers argued they were able to "really see" their children as individuals, rather than as racialized bodies. This has been a popular position, especially among whites. However, in a racialized society in which race *does* matter, socially and materially for people, not "seeing" race has also been equated to indifference—to not seeing inequality structured along the lines of race (Newfield and Gordon 1996, 89).

The majority of China-adoptive mothers argue that the visible racial difference of their children (from whites) must be acknowledged, and that it is this difference itself that necessitates cultural engagement. The influence of multiculturalism, which demands the acknowledgment and celebration of ethnic difference, can be seen in this perspective. For example, Eloise Nolan shared with me that participating in Chinese culture was obligatory for her daughters "because it is their culture. When they look in the mirror, they can see that they're different and they know that they're from China, that they're Chinese." This primordial view of ethnicity, which posits ethnic identity as innate and natural (not socially constructed), was common among China-adoptive mothers. They argued that their children *must* engage with Chinese culture because they look Chinese and because looking Chinese is *different,* such that people will hold the expectation that their children are familiar with Chinese culture. Leanne Becker, who adopted two girls from China, said that strangers expect her daughters "to have a set of experiences. And I think life is a lot easier if you look like who you are; if on the outside what people can expect of you is what you expect of yourself."

This primordial view of ethnicity fixes ethnic identity to the child. By virtue of the child's phenotype and birthplace, she becomes ethnic: she embodies ethnicity. In this model, ethnicity and race are intricately intertwined: the darker the skin, the more "exotic" the place of birth, the deeper the ethnic identity; likewise, the lighter the skin, the more provincial the place of the birth, the more superficial the ethnicity. Therefore, for whites, the racial marking of ethnicity is largely subtle and hidden to the practitioner; for nonwhites it is visible and salient.

Asian Americans often experience the expectation of authentic primordial ethnicity based on phenotype. In her research on later-generation (East) Asian Americans, Mia Tuan (1998) found many of her respondents continually confronting the belief in public that they were ethnic—more ethnic than they were American; that, based on phenotype alone, they were competent in Korean, Chinese, or Japanese culture, and fluent in the language of their ancestors.

Tuan argues that, due to these "ethnic expectations," ethnicity continues to play a salient role in the lives of Asian Americans despite their economic assimilation and long-term residence in the United States (going back four or five generations). Tuan connects this to race-based ideas of who constitutes Americans and foreigners and argues that the ethnic expectation is one way in which even seemingly fully "assimilated" American groups are racially Othered.

Studies have found contemporary Asian Americans sometimes deemphasizing their Korean (or Chinese, Japanese, etcetera) ethnic practices in order to hasten their acceptance into the white-dominated American mainstream (Kibria 2002a; Tuan 1998). This mirrors earlier Americanization efforts in which immigrants (Asians included) were effectively forced to abandon or subvert ethnic cultural practices in favor of white mainstream ones. Those efforts, examined in such books as Noel Ignatiev's *How the Irish Became White* (1996), were "successful" for earlier generations of white ethnics in that various white ethnic groups (the Irish, Italians, Jews) transitioned from ethnic "Other" to white American. For Asian Americans and other racial minority groups, the "Americanization" efforts were stymied by phenotype. Furthermore, due to the way Asian Americans are "racialized ethnics," in that their race signals ethnicity, they do not actually have to even engage in ethnic culture in order to experience an assumption of foreignness (Kibria 2002a; Waters 1990). As Tuan states, "An ethnic identity is imposed on them by virtue of their physical appearance" (Tuan 1998, 28).

China-adoptive mothers seem largely unaware of the ethnic Othering of Asians that occurs through expectations for cultural competency. Mothers held the belief that Asians in the United States do practice ethnicity and, moreover, that they *should* practice ethnicity. They anticipated others would hold similar beliefs about their daughters and that this was reason to keep culture.

This view of ethnicity not only fixes "culture" to the child, but it fixes the notion of "culture" as well. "Chinese culture" itself is viewed as a particular set of traditional practices (holidays, foods, language) that is stable and unchanging and can therefore be accessed by adoptive parents who are dedicated and vigilant enough to draw from it. The irony is that Chinese culture is not fixed but is dynamic and changing, just like all other cultures (see Louie 2008). Even that which is understood to be "traditional culture" is read and reinscribed through contemporary eyes (Nagel 1994).

But culture keeping, heavily influenced by multiculturalism, largely depends on perceiving "culture" as fixed and stable. This idea of fixed culture is not uniquely held by adoptive parents, of course, but is an important framing of culture more generally. Ideas about what properly constitutes "authentic" Chinese culture proliferate, even, as Andrea Louie tells us, among Chinese Americans (2008). Those ideas are used to distinguish and cast value between "real" and "Americanized" cultural practices or items.

In an interesting twist, however, China-adoptive mothers also framed cultural engagement as a set of practices that can allow adoptees to have choices about their ethnic identities. Facilitating Chinese connections for her daughters, Leanne Becker argued, was also based on the belief that "you need to be able to choose whether you want to be the kind of person people expect you to be or not. And they can only choose that if they have these experiences." Mothers saw culture keeping as a way of providing children choices for the future of how they would like to identify ethnically. Nancy Thorne thought it was important to encourage her daughter to engage with Chinese culture in order for her to have options in the future: "I want Abigail to learn Chinese even when, say, she doesn't want to learn Chinese, so she can have a choice there. And so that when she goes through all the changes she will go through, she does have choices."

In this model of flexible ethnicity, Chinese identity is framed as one of several (or many) identities available for internationally adopted children from China. This approach to ethnicity closely parallels the "symbolic ethnicity" model of later generation white ethnics in that ethnicity is seen as "a personal choice of whether to be ethnic at all, and, for an increasing majority of people, of which ethnicity to be" (Gans 1979; Waters 1990, 147). Some China-adoptive mothers implied ethnicity was something they could engage their children in today but which their children could "opt out" of in the future. As children, participants argued, Chinese adoptees should practice culture so that they will be able to choose to pursue a salient Chinese identity *or not* when they are older.

It is an interesting contrast between these two views of ethnicity. Ethnicity is primordial and, therefore, must be engaged in because the children are racialized Others: they look Chinese, and others will expect them to behave as Chinese (and to have a certain cultural repertoire). At the same time, ethnicity is optional: it is one part of their identity that they may decide to activate or engage in the future if they so desire. Ethnicity is seen by these mothers at one and the same time as both primordial/fixed/necessary *and* malleable/constructed/optional.

Culture keeping offers a comfortable avenue for mothers to address this "double-bind" of racialized ethnicity (Dorow 2006a, 205–6). In culture keeping, China-adoptive mothers fulfill the ethnic expectation they place on their children based on racial difference, yet the cultural practices themselves are loose enough that they can easily be slipped on or off. Culture keeping is posed by China-adoptive mothers as not only the best way to address race for their families, but, in essence, the *only* way many know how do to so.

The framing of culture keeping as an integral and necessary part of international-adoptive family life due to racism and racial identity issues does not translate well for families with children from Russia. Some Russia-adoptive parents, however, have incorporated a multicultural perspective into their approach to international-adoptive parenting. Culture keeping, these women argue, is an important aspect of mothering their children as it helps to ensure healthy self-esteem in their adopted children. While China-adoptive mothers were similarly concerned with the self-esteem of their children, the exact foci of their discussions on this topic differed.

Although the children in the China- and- Russia-adoptive families in this study were all adopted as infants or toddlers (as was a requirement for participation in the study) and had, therefore, spent roughly similar amounts of time in institutionalized care, Russia-adoptive mothers expressed more concerns regarding the *emotional* repercussions of institutionalization per se than did China-adoptive mothers. I see this as related to the varying circumstances involved in the placement of children into state care from China and Russia. China-adoptive mothers understood the Chinese state as the main instigator for abandonment in China. They argued that the one-child policy and cultural preference for boys led to, in essence, forced abandonment. This framing absolves birth mothers of agency or responsibility in the abandonment act. In this narrative, China birth mothers remain pure victims, as the Chinese state itself is held responsible for the abandonment of children.

Russia-adoptive mothers, on the other hand, have no corresponding social institution on which to place responsibility for their children's institutionalization. While they spoke of the constraints of poverty, responsibility was placed squarely on the birth mothers' shoulders. As a result, Russia-adoptive mothers were motivated to keep Russian culture as a way to balance what they saw as early negative rejection by birth mothers and to instill pride in their children regarding their early lives.

Central to Russia-adoptive mothers' narratives regarding their motivations for culture keeping was the moment when the adopted child realizes that she was abandoned (or relinquished) by a birth mother. In his popular work on contemporary adoption, Adam Pertman writes, "it can be a confusing, painful revelation" when children "start to internalize a fact they might have known but never really understood: that, in order for their parents to have gotten them, someone had to give them up" (2000, 84). Culture keeping among Russian culture keepers was an active strategy to deal with the moment of realized rejection and mitigate the feelings of shame and loss by helping their children feel good about who they are. As Kerry Mead explained it to me, when adopted children ask themselves, "Why did my birth mother let me go? Wasn't I good enough?" adoptive mothers should help their children gain self-confidence by keeping culture which makes them "proud of where they're from and the culture that they came from."

All adoption, regardless of type, involves some type of loss: the loss of the birth family for the child and birth parent(s), and, for those who desired one, the loss of a biological child for the adoptive parent(s) (Franklin 1998; Loux 1997; Modell 1994, 2002; Rothman 2005). Russian culture keeping was explicitly about the absent birth mother. The loss that Russia-adoptive mothers spoke of trying to fill for their children through culture keeping is the loss of kinship, the loss of the first mother.

Women with children from China also engage in culture keeping to mediate loss. While they acknowledged the benefits of being adopted into a family in the United States, participants characterized the removal from China as a "huge loss" for the child. They most often characterized this loss as centering on China and Chinese culture, not on birth mothers. Eloise Nolan stated, "I was very sad and cried a lot to think that I was taking her away from her culture and everything she knew." Priscilla Anderson felt that the move to the United States resulted in "stripping her [daughter] of her culture."

Mothers attempt to give their children positive aspects of China to appreciate in order to, as Lorraine Burg stated, "offset the sadness and the hurt and anger they are going to feel about being abandoned." (Re)introducing culture into their children's lives was a way to attempt restitution. Doing so was seen as a distinct mothering duty; as Lynn Werden framed it, "I feel that pain for her and feel like it's my challenge to do something with it. Like make some bridges across that place." In keeping culture, they hoped to give their children "positive pieces from the same culture that abandoned them, so that it's not [all] negative."

The mothers in this study with children from China spoke of the international adoption process as creating a break or chasm in the child's ethnic identity. Culture keeping was seen as a way to "make some bridges" by connecting the child to this interrupted ethnic identity and, in doing so, establish positive feelings about China and self with the hope of alleviating some of the pain resulting from abandonment and separation from China.

Women with children from Russia did not frame adoption in this way. For Russia-adoptive mothers, the child's identity does not suffer a disruption due to their leave of Russia. Rather, the Russia-adoptive mothers located the source of potential pain for their children in the abandonment by birth mothers.

This distinction results in adoptive mothers experiencing varying levels of guilt for removing their children from their countries of origin. Mothers with children from China expressed unease about their role in separating their children from China and in the resulting loss or pain that they imagine their children will experience. This theme, consistently articulated in my conversations with China-adoptive mothers, was strikingly absent from my interviews with Russia-adoptive mothers.

In their narratives, China-adoptive mothers posed Chinese culture keeping as an active, positive strategy to help make amends for their role in separating their children from their heritage. Culture keeping was therefore not only viewed in and of itself as something positive for the child, but also as a strategy to help China-adoptive mothers come to terms with their own feelings of guilt.

In contrast, Russia-adoptive mothers did not speak of guilt due to their role in removing their children from Russia. In fact, several told me that through adoption they literally had saved their children from certain death due to failing health and malnutrition; a sentiment none of the China adopters expressed (even those who spoke of the seriously ill health status of their children when adopted).

While the loss of "authentic" culture propels culture keeping among China-adoptive families, those with children from Russia focus on the loss of the "authentic" birth mother or family—and often a very specific person. It was not unusual for the Russia-adoptive families in my sample to have identifying information about the birth mothers (and sometimes the birth fathers) of their children. Some parents had enough information to be able to sketch out the reasons their child was relinquished or abandoned. Some had even established contact with birth parents. While most Russia-adoptive parents in my sample have not shared these facts (or hunches) in detail with their children (especially if there are siblings who were not relinquished for adoption), they are nonetheless painful for parents.

Culture keeping was a way for Russia-adoptive mothers to engage positively with the child's original history and present the child with a positive birth mother image, steeped in authentic ethnic practices. In this framework, "Mother Russia" was a figurative mother (warm, embracing, dynamic) who, in effect, stood in place for an actual mother, the absent birth mother. Participants saw the birth mother and Russia as intricately entwined, with negative feelings about one necessarily spilling over into negative feelings about the other. Culture keeping was a strategy to help children think positively about their birth mothers (and their own relationship to them) through engaging in positive ways with Russian culture. This can be seen in the way Christina Denison, who adopted from Russia after experiencing secondary infertility, spoke about her daughter: "From the reading I've done, a lot of internationally adopted children tend to view their country almost as their birth mother, especially if there's no contact. And if they do that, then I think that it's essential that the view of their birth country be balanced and as positive as it can be because that's who they are. That's where they came from. Just as my son came from me, Oksana came from Russia, and that's important."

Russia-adoptive mothers work to ensure that their children had a least a superficial understanding—at an age appropriate level—of the larger social context of abandonment and relinquishment of children in Russia. As detailed earlier, child neglect in Russia is currently at crisis proportions, with the country leading the world in the number of children abandoned (ARO 2005). The dramatic social and economic changes since the fall of Communism, which have caused widespread unemployment, have had a devastating impact on Russia's children. The resulting increase in family violence, alcohol and drug addiction, and disease (particularly HIV and other sexually transmitted diseases) has led to more children without parental care, living on the street or in state institutions (Steltzner 2003). Russia-adoptive mothers explain this social context to their children in an attempt to ease the sting of abandonment. Carol Acher spoke of how important it was for Russian adoptees to understand the constraints placed on birth parents in Russia. She argued that if the children "can understand the culture then, that single parenting isn't okay there or it's not feasible . . . that . . . these people do this because they want something better for their children than they can provide" then they "shouldn't feel that they come from a bad country, a bad place." Working on the understanding children have of Russia and their feelings about their birth mothers through participation in Russian culture was not only viewed as a way to link the children to their past, but as a way to cultivate an essential piece of their children's very being. These mothers' perspectives were echoed in Christina Denison's words when she said,

"I absolutely believe that my daughter's heritage is part of who she is." Russian ethnicity was understood as an intrinsic part of the child's identity. Cultivating that identity through engagement with Russian culture, these women believed, helped to ensure a positive and healthy self-image for their children.

Conclusion

The encouragement of ethnic socialization has become standard practice in the adoption world. Culture is marketed and celebrated as one of the joys and obligations of international adoptive parenting. It is part of the way all international-adoptive programs are packaged, made appealing, and sold to adoptive parents. However, as this chapter has detailed, there are real differences in how adoptive mothers with racial minority children and those with white children experience the call to ethnic socialization and understand their own culture keeping motivations. Women with racial minority children receive stronger edicts and support to engage in culture in the process of adopting their children. This difference in the early stages of the life of these families sheds light on the mothers' varied positions vis-à-vis racial, ethnic, and kinship ideologies that undergird articulated motivations to keep culture.

Culture keeping is overwhelmingly propelled by the position that ethnic socialization is required for the healthy self-esteem of international adoptees. Mothers rely on two notions to support this position. The first is the psychosocial idea that adoptees suffer from adoption-related loss. By engaging in culture, mothers hope to positively reconnect their children to that which they lost through abandonment and adoption. China-adoptive mothers center their attention on the loss of authentic Chinese culture while Russia-adoptive mothers focus on the loss of birth kin. By engaging in culture keeping, mothers hope their children would make positive connections to their culture and kin in order to facilitate healthy notions of who they are, where they came from, and the family they have "forever" joined.

The second notion supporting the idea that ethnic socialization is required for the healthy self-esteem of adoptees is multiculturalism, which demands the acknowledgment and celebration of racial and ethnic identity. Both China- and Russia-adoptive mothers who keep culture view ethnicity as primordial and fixed to their children through place of birth. Engaging their children in birth culture is seen, therefore, to express an inherent part of their children's identity: the children were born in China or Russia and, therefore, should practice their culture of birth.

The ideologies of multiculturalism and adoption loss demand culture keeping from all international-adoptive mothers. Race, however—specifically racial minority status—also plays a large role in the push to keep culture. For the China-adoptive mothers in my sample, this was expressed in the "ethnic expectation" (Tuan 1998) mothers held that Asian Americans embody—and should be encouraged to express—a deeper cultural connection than others. They felt their Chinese-born children should be able to meet this expectation, and they attempted to ensure this through ethnic socialization.

Chinese culture keeping was also motivated by the fear of racism. Like biological mothers of color, those with adopted Chinese children used engagement with culture as a strategy to counter the negative images and experiences they imagine their children will incur due to their racial minority status. Unlike mothers of color, however, China-adoptive mothers had had little experience with racial identity issues or racism prior to mothering.

These understandings of race (that ethnicity is expected of racial minority children and that its practice is an antidote to racism) place more intense pressure on China-adoptive mothers to engage in the ethnic socialization of their children. Because these ideologies are used as the general framing for culture keeping in the adoption industry and community, adoptive mothers with white children are given more leeway in the choices they make around ethnic socialization. As will be explored in the following chapters, it also leaves mothers of white children without the strong support for culture keeping that those with children of color experience.

This pressure or support to engage in culture keeping among Chinese adopters, however, is tempered or complicated by another framing. Caught in a "double-bind" (Dorow 2006a), many China-adoptive mothers understood ethnicity to be at one and the same time primordial *and* malleable. Culture keeping is seen as necessary due to place of birth and phenotype, but it can also give children "ethnic options" (Waters 1990), choices for the future on how they wish to identify.

As this chapter has explored, the motivations to keep culture among China and Russia-adoptive mothers vary some among each group, but, due to ideas of race and culture, they differ more so between them. The following chapters explore how the ideologies of race, culture, and ethnicity which mothers articulate in sharing their motivations to keep culture shape the actual practices in which they engage their families and the privileges and constraints they experience in doing so.

4

Negotiating and Normalizing Difference

In the late 1990s, international-adoptive parents began pressuring the U.S. government to change the citizenship requirements for their foreign-born children. At the time, these children had to undergo the standard process of naturalization for immigrants. They were admitted to the United States on immigrant visas, and their new parents had to apply to the Immigration and Naturalization Service (INS) for permanent residency ("green cards") and certificates of citizenship on their behalf. The total processing time from immigrant to citizen sometimes took up to several years because of paperwork backlogs at the INS. Children occasionally "fell through the cracks" and reached the age of majority without American citizenship having been established (U.S. Congress 2000).

In 2000, two bills were presented before Congress in hopes of changing the law. The Adopted Orphans Citizenship Act (H.R. 2883), the more radical of the two, pushed for children to be granted retroactive U.S. citizenship going back to the time of their birth, in effect legally erasing the existence of the child's birth parents and prior citizenship in his or her birth country. The second bill, the Child Citizenship Act (H.R. 3667), which eventually became law (Child Citizenship Act of 2000, Public Law 106–395), asked for children to be granted automatic citizenship when they enter the United States with their new adoptive parents (Leiter, McDonald, and Jacobson 2006).

The citizenship issue and the arguments used for passage of the Child Citizenship Act touch on key themes in the lives of international adoptive families. They speak to the way adoptive parents think about the national and racial identities of their children. They focus on legal and social recognition of adoptive families and parents' exclusive "ownership" of adopted children despite the fact that those children "belonged" to others (birth parents and countries) before them.

The discourse surrounding these citizenship proceedings reflects a certain entitlement in both how parents think about themselves and the children they adopt and certain resulting prerogatives regarding institutional interactions involving their families. Many adoptive parents felt that the citizenship requirements were not only redundant (many of the same papers had to be first filed with the INS for the immigrant visa and adoption) and burdensome but *unfair.* Maureen Evans, then Executive Director of the Joint Council on International Children's Services, wrote in a statement given before Congress that "this legislation being considered today, HR 2883, recognizes that adopted children of U.S. citizens are entitled to the same treatment under the law as children born to U.S. citizens. This is fair and just. Adoptive families should have the same legal rights and privileges as any other family" (U.S. Congress 2000, 33).

Maureen Evans was, of course, not referring to just "any other family" but to a specific kind of family. She was not, for example, referring to immigrant families who must file permanent residency paperwork and apply for certificates of citizenship on behalf of their children. Nor was she referring to children born to American citizens abroad, some of whom, at the time, also had to file citizenship paperwork. These families also have to endure the arduous bureaucracy of the INS (now U.S. Citizenship and Immigration Services) and the long delays that accompany any dealings with them. Moreover, they are often subject to immigration paperwork and proceedings without the English fluency, American cultural understandings, and economic resources that American adoptive parents have that make dealing with Immigration Services easier. The "any other family" Maureen Evans brought to mind was the family many adoptive parents would have had if they had given birth to a biological child: a white, middle-class family of birthright American citizens—in essence, the privileged "American Family."

The "American Family"

Despite the existence of a great diversity of family forms in the United States—in cultural representations, public discourse, many social institutions, and in everyday interactions—the "American Family" is often posited as a nuclear unit of heterosexual, married parents and their biological children (Wegar 1997; Hansen 2005). The "American Family" is also presented in popular culture and much scholarly work as "white, Euro-American, [and] middle-class" (Garey and Hansen 1998, xvii); it is almost always monoracial. These ideological understandings of the family and kinship are privileged in the United States despite the fact that not everyone "participates in identical sorts of kinship relations [nor] subscribes to one universally agreed-upon definition of the family" (Weston 1991, 22). There is a delay between the shift in family forms and kinship relations and the shift in social recognition of and institutional support for those new families. There is progress, of course. More diverse family forms are seen, for example, in the mainstream media. However, dominant cultural understandings of the family have not totally caught up with the diversity of family forms or functioning we have today in the United States (Pyke 2000).

Dorothy Smith calls the idealized family the Standard North American Family (SNAF), and she argues that this "ideological code," which includes a gendered division of labor (with a breadwinning father and stay-at-home mother), infiltrates public policy and political practice (1993). Laws governing marriage and adoption, for example, have historically benefited white, monoracial, heterosexual families. This is changing; however, those privileges linger. The "American Family" is more, therefore, than just an idea. It translates into macrostructural forces that directly impact our experiences living in families.

The idea of the "American Family" also translates into the symbolic privileging of particular family forms over others. One way in which this can be seen is that families who do not match this norm—poor and working-class families, racial or ethnic minority families, interracial families, families with homosexual parents, families without children, divorced or remarried "blended" families, and single parent families—are often discredited in popular culture and framed as dysfunctional, deficient, or "unique" and worthy of special attention and interest.

Mothers who have families who match the cultural representation of the "American Family" are afforded special privileges in the United States. As middle-class persons, they have an economic stability relative to poor and working-class mothers (Lareau 2003); they do not have the same worries about how to feed, shelter, or clothe their children (DeVault 1991; Zollar 1985). They find representations of themselves and their children easily in popular culture, and they find their family form supported in daily interactions in public (McIntosh 1988). Unlike mothers of children of color, they do not have to concern themselves with educating their children on how to survive in a racially stratified society (Carothers 1998; Collins 1994; Uttal 1998). While they indeed have a multitude of concerns for their children, basic necessities, access to cultural representations which represent their families, societal support for their family form, and racial safety are not among them.

White mothers of biological white children also enjoy a large degree of flexibility in the choices they make around ethnicity. Due to the history of a high degree of intermarriage between whites of various ethnic heritages, white mothers of biological white children can choose which ethnicity among the many in their family genealogy to celebrate or ignore (Waters 1990). They are not pressured to engage in public ethnic competency exercises such as are foisted upon Asian Americans (Tuan 1998). White mothers of biological white children have wide leverage in terms of ethnic identity development and participation. In essence, they are free to enjoy a "symbolic ethnicity" (Gans 1979; Waters 1990).

The participants in my study—white middle-class mothers with children adopted internationally—have access to some but not all of these same privileges. Through adopting and parenting their children (including applying for citizenship), mothers with children from China and Russia confront the "American Family" and the gap between their own families and that dominant ideal. This chapter examines how mothers with children from China and those with children from Russia negotiate and normalize that gap through culture keeping.

Inclusion and Difference

The themes of difference, desire, belonging, and bifurcation saturate the world of international adoption. In adoption discourse, from the parents' perspective, two life stages are conceived: pre-adoption, there is the "waiting family" and the "waiting child" who become the "forever family" on "gotcha day" when the child is received.[1] Children belong to a "birth family" and then to a "forever family." There is the mother who bore the child and the one (or two or more) who will raise her. There are two nations, two cultures and, often, two races involved in the process.

The adopted child herself is seen to be both object and subject in this process (Dorow 2006a). She is seen to both experience these changes (the shift between countries, between families, between "waiting" and "forever") and to represent them. As she moves between countries, she is seen to transform. She first "belongs" to one context and then to another: to one family and culture and nation and then to another. She is seen to embody this bifurcated history and to have, therefore, a bifurcated identity. This is largely how adoptive mothers spoke of their children: as both "American" and as "Chinese," both "Russian" and "American."

In this framing of national identities, America/China and America/Russia are conceptualized as corresponding monolithic entities with corresponding sets of cultural practices that have little overlap. Cultural activities themselves are framed as "Chinese" or "American," as "Russian" or "American." This can be seen in the remarks made by Astrid Tucker about her Chinese-born daughter: "Sometimes she's interested in stuff that's Chinese and sometimes she doesn't want to be Chinese, I think. She wants to be American." As Astrid's comments shows, children themselves are seen as "American" *or* as "Chinese," as "American" *or* as "Russian." Some speak of the children as "American" *and* "Chinese," or "American" *and* "Russian," but even then, these are seen as distinct identities co-residing in the child. Parents in my study very rarely spoke of their children as "Chinese American" or "Russian American." Mothers reserved the "Chinese American" and "Russian American" nomenclatures largely for who they referred to as "real" Chinese Americans or Russian Americans (i.e., non-adoptive immigrants or their descendents). Although, ironically, they did speak of their families as "Chinese American" or "Russian American," reflecting, the "marriage" of "Chinese" (or "Russian") children with "American" parents. Richard Tessler et al. (1999) employ the term "American Chinese" for China-adoptive families to highlight the American and Chinese aspects of China-adoptive families and to distinguish them from "Chinese Americans," but none of the mothers in my sample referred to themselves as such.

The framing of bifurcated national and cultural identities both mirrors and challenges how the transition from birth to adoptive parents has historically been conceptualized as a complete and clean break from the past. In the "clean break" model, most popular in the first half of the twentieth century, adoptive parents symbolically replace birth parents (Melosh 2002). Birth parents were figuratively erased out of existence. They were not talked about or thought of as the first parents of the child. Children's birth certificates were legally doctored, with the birth parents' names removed and replaced by those of the adoptive parents.

The "clean break" model was visible in the early years of international adoption as well, when the cultural and racial identities of the children were "removed" and "replaced" by those of the adoptive parents (Volkman 2005, 85). As Barbara Yngvesson writes, "The clean break separates the child from everything that constitutes her grounds for belonging to this family and this nation while establishing her transferability to that family and that nation. With a past that has been cut away—an old identity that no longer exists—the child can be re-embedded in a new place, almost as though she never moved at all" (2004, 168).

Much of the work adult domestic and international adoptees (and birth mothers) have enacted around the issue of adoption has been complicating the picture of a "clean break" from the past, on reclaiming their origins and stories, and reconnecting to their "birth" families, nations, and cultures. Adult international adoptees argue that although they were transferred from one nation to another, their origins and the differences constructed about them remain (especially those due to phenotype) (see Trenka et al. 2006). Those differences not only remain, but adoptees have demanded they be acknowledged.

Influenced by adoption activists and changes in adoption practice (i.e., the movement toward open records and open triad relationships), the contemporary adoption industry and community now encourage adoptive parents to hold adoptees' origin information (including details from their particular histories and cultural facts and goods) in trust for their children. A market has even opened for investigating and gathering this information. A China-adoptive parent, for example, can hire someone to track down the foster parents who cared for her child in China, to research the site at which the child was abandoned and discovered, and to locate the (legally required) newspaper ad announcing the discovery (following abandonment) of the child.

Although openness and communication about difference is now professionally prescribed, the "clean break" model continues to influence contemporary adoption discourse. On adoption blogs, electronic mailing lists, and memoirs, contemporary adoptive parents write of "completing their family" (and the process of adopting) through "bringing their child home"—as if that home was always the child's and the child had simply been misplaced. This is, in fact, how family formation through adoption is sometimes explained to adoptees. Children are told that they "got lost on their way from heaven," for example, and that their (adoptive) parents needed to find them in order to bring them to their true, intended destination.

There is a tension between the clean break from the past,

which allows adoptive parents a feeling of complete proprietary memory of the child, and the acknowledgment of difference, which lays open the adoptive family to other histories, memories, and families. Culture keeping is posed as an instrument—perhaps *the* instrument—to heal this rift, to address race, address difference, mitigate future family conflict (especially that which arises in adolescence), and work through family issues. Culture keeping is intended to allow for the acknowledgment of the child's specific and unique origins while doing so in a way that does not necessarily jeopardize the feeling of exclusive kinship adoptive parents crave.

Parents also frame culture keeping, however, as a mechanism through which difference can actually be highlighted or reinforced for their children, rather than normalized. Some parents argue that the culture keeping "solution"—the panacea to dealing with difference, in essence—is itself a problem. This tension between culture keeping as problem and culture keeping as solution is expressed in an anxiety about finding the correct balance between difference (of child and parent and of child and community) and inclusion (of the child in the family and of the family in the community).

This "balancing act" was the biggest challenge mothers reported in keeping culture for their children. It was expressed as a careful choreographed dance in deciding upon and implementing both appropriate kinds and appropriate amounts of birth culture socialization in the lives of their families. Part of this dilemma was simple logistics. Like many mothers, especially those who are engaged in full-time professional employment, the women in my study were in considerable "time binds" when it came to scheduling and keeping up with the various activities of their families (see also Garey 1995; Hansen 2005; Hochschild 1997).

The time bind exists for several reasons. It is partly due to "fast capitalism": the way in which daily life has sped up, boundaries between work and home life have become blurred, and private time has been reduced in postmodern capitalist societies (Agger 1989 and 2004; Agger and Shelton 2007). Culture keeping sometimes unintentionally falls victim to the resulting time conflicts. Russia-adoptive mother Judy Inman expressed her inability to engage with culture keeping explicitly as a consequence of work and family demands: "You know, with two kids and a full-time job, I just—there are probably other things I would do [with Russian culture] if I were home more, but I just don't have the time to do it."

Mothers also faced a time bind because of a particular middle-class style of childrearing that demands high parental involvement in all aspects of the child's life. Annette Lareau calls this parenting style "concerted cultivation," in which parents attempt to "stimulate their children's development and foster their cognitive and social skills" through management of the minutiae of children's lives (2003, 5). An important aspect of concerted cultivation is high levels of child participation in extracurricular activities (dance, music, sports, chess) overseen by adults that are meant to help facilitate children's emotional, social, intellectual, and physical development.

While the women in my study, like many middle-class parents today, appeared to ascribe to concerted cultivation as a necessary component of raising well-rounded children, it was taxing for them to oversee the number of involved activities (including school, homework, play dates, and doctor's visits, as well as enrichment programs) in which most of their children were involved. To emphasize how challenging it was simply to coordinate parents' and children's schedules, China-adoptive mother Holly Pritchard showed me an elaborate color-coded weekly schedule for her family written on a large poster board. Each minute of the day, *literally*, was accounted for. It was an amazing jumble of colors designating school and work, music lessons, swimming, martial arts, Chinese language classes, homework, rest time, sleep, and eating. Holly, who was a single mother of one child, handled this impressive schedule (and the making of the elaborate calendar) in order to keep herself and her daughter on top of their many activities. While not all middle-class professional women create weekly poster boards to manage family activities, time constraints and hectic schedules are an established component of contemporary middle-class mothering.

For adoptive mothers, finding time for culture keeping was made even more difficult because many activities for children tend to be held at similar times (Saturday mornings, for example). Therefore, mothers put time and thought into the choice of specific activities. They had only a few key time slots during each week that were free from children's school commitments and their own work demands in which to schedule extracurricular activities. In those free periods, women who kept culture had to figure out how to incorporate culture keeping activities (such as play dates with other adoptive families, dance or language classes, and FCC or FRUA events) and other types of extracurricular activities they found important or enjoyable for their children, such as swimming or music lessons. Mothers are often forced, therefore, to select between culture keeping and other extracurricular activities. China-adoptive mother Rachel Abramson spoke of this dilemma: "One of the struggles we've had is how much do you do of each and how can you do both? She takes Chinese dance on Saturdays so she can't do Shabbat or go to Hebrew school because we do this. So, do we do Chinese? Do we do Jewish? Is it too hard to do both?"

These are the questions that swirl around culture keeping: how much ethic socialization is enough? How do you balance culture keeping with other activities and other forms of child socialization? This topic is openly addressed by adoptive mothers. China-adoptive mother Stacey Dita told me that, among her friends with children adopted from China, "there's a lot of talk about how much we do, do we do too much? How much is okay?" The decisions made by China- and Russia-adoptive mothers regarding these issues reflect more than concern about time management and the imperative of concerted cultivation. It was in these culture keeping decisions that mothers attempted to normalize their families by balancing certain identities for their children vis-à-vis others in their social worlds.

The Balancing Act

The concern about balancing inclusion and difference was demonstrated in several ways. First, there was a fear articulated by mothers regarding overemphasizing birth culture in their families' lives—of pushing their children too much into a position of difference within their surrounding social milieu.

The heart of this issue of "going overboard" with culture is a concern for creating balance between what mothers see as various components of their children's identities that include them or exclude them from familial and American identities. As China-adoptive mother Shannon Lynch said, "These kids were born in China but they're being raised in America. They are Americans, and they should be Americans first." Most mothers were dedicated to the inclusion of birth culture. However, they spoke of their children's "Chinese-ness" or "Russian-ness" as something that could set their children apart from their neighbors, classmates, and nuclear and extended family members. They wanted their children to enjoy their birth ethnicity, but not to the point where it excluded them from connecting to others and enjoying similar activities to those people who largely composed their social worlds.

Mothers argued that an "obsession" with birth culture would be detrimental to their children. Many referred to other adoptive families who took the incorporation of birth culture to an extreme. China-adoptive mother Astrid Tucker said, "Some people, their houses are like from Chinatown; to my way of thinking, that's too much, going overboard." In order to avoid "going overboard," mothers sought to normalize participation in cultural activities. They wanted their children to enjoy being Chinese or Russian. Yet they did not want the Chinese-ness or Russian-ness of their children to infringe on their status as "Americans." They want their children to be Chinese or Russian, but not *too* Chinese or Russian. China-adoptive mother Shannon Lynch explained, "I don't want them to think that they're so different. We're a family. We're a family that came together under different circumstances than other families. But a lot of times in a kid's mind 'different' is 'bad' and I don't want them to ever get that connotation."

There were some mothers, particularly among those with children from Russia, for whom the fear of difference represented in "going overboard" was so strong that they largely avoided culture keeping. These women wanted their children, as Linda Grashi put it, to "be treated the same way" as other children in their communities. Although they spoke of themselves as fairly committed to culture keeping, in our discussions it became clear that they felt in and of itself that culture keeping was "going overboard" and would ensure that the adopted status of their children would be highlighted. This, they reported, would lead to their children being singled out and possibly ostracized. They were concerned that even minimal exposure to birth culture would stigmatize their children. Russia-adoptive mother Amanda Holmquist, for example, explained the limitations she placed on culture keeping for her daughter: "There is exposure [to Russian culture]. For instance, Christmas ornaments—she'll get Russian ornaments. She had a Russian stocking. Different things like that. So when I see

something or do something it's neat, it's not atypical or different or selling her out."

Amanda's concern that Russian practices be normalized—
safely contained within the home, nonpublic, and not "atypical
or different"—was common among Russia-adoptive mothers.
As part of not "making a big deal out of" their child's Russian-
ness, some women let their children dictate the degree to which
Russian culture would be a part of their lives. The thoughts of
Michelle Russo were typical: "Initially I was going to be doing
all this stuff. I wanted them to know their heritage and all this
stuff and it would be fun to go back and forth. I've really let
the kids kind of move me in that—if they've showed an interest
in it, then we'll follow it. But most of the time they're like, 'Can
I go on PlayStation? Can we go to the beach?' "

Child-led culture keeping was rare among women with
children from China. The emphasis on culture keeping as a
strategy for dealing with racial issues did not allow for many
China-adoptive mothers to let their children determine the
amount of cultural engagement in their families. Several
China-adoptive mothers, however, did share the outlook that
children's desires and interests should shape culture keeping.
For example, when I asked China-adoptive mother Shirley
McIntosh what role Chinese culture plays in her family's life,
she responded, "Well, it doesn't play as much as I'd like it to
'cause [my daughter] for many years rejected it. She didn't want
nothing to do with it." Shirley said, "I wouldn't say we emphasize so much the birth stuff but we talk about whatever it is she
wants to talk about. I'm of the philosophy—and I've gotten
this advice from the experts—that whatever she asks about to
answer in a sort of simple way. If she wants more, she'll ask
for more. So, you know, we haven't gotten that much involved
with the Chinese culture yet only to the extent that she seems
accepting of it; like I don't ever push anything. So I feel like I
give her what she wants to be given. And getting immersed in

her own family structure today seems more important for her than—but, you know, it will evolve, I'm sure."

With little parental encouragement or identification with birth culture, it is not surprising that the children of these women show little interest in cultural activities and scant connection to China or Russia. Even more highly culturally involved mothers, however, still feared that their children would resist the cultural practices that they were trying to "foist" upon them. Women often used examples of other families as cautionary tales when talking about the potential for a child-initiated backlash to cultural activities. China-adoptive mother Priscilla Anderson shared how a Korea-adoptive family served as an example for her:

Other people I talked to who had Korean kids who were slightly older said they had three Korean daughters and she said, "We shoved Korea down their throats for about six years. By the time they were finally able to tell us, you know, they started saying, "I don't want to wear those clothes." They started saying "Enough with the Korean stuff. We don't want to know all the Korean stuff!" And they started rejecting it. So then I said, "Was it all worth it?" I mean, I don't know. Maybe they have a background but she said they made a huge effort to go to every Korean Day that they could think of and by the end, the kids didn't want to be different.

The fear of "going overboard" with culture keeping, and being rejected by their children in the process, was tempered by the additional fear of doing *too little* to best properly transmit cultural information or to integrate birth country culture into their families' lives. To engage in "too little" culture keeping was seen as taboo. Mothers equated it to another "cardinal sin" in the contemporary adoption world: deliberately hiding the fact of adoption. Most women, therefore, also expressed a concern that they were not doing enough regarding culture.

Mothers were concerned about both "going overboard" and doing "too little" with birth culture because of the actual impact it would have on their children. If the proper balance was not instituted, mothers were fearful that their children's self-esteem and healthy social development would be negatively impacted. Women were also concerned that an inappropriate level of culture keeping would impact how they were perceived by other adoptive parents. The idea that other people would find them either "obsessed" with birth culture or, on the other end of the spectrum, "totally Americanized," shaped how mothers engaged in culture keeping. In this way, culture keeping can be understood in the larger context of an ideology of "intensive mothering" that assesses "good mothers" and "bad mothers" along the lines of how closely women engage in a type of mothering that is "child-centered, expert-guided, emotionally absorbing, labor intensive, and financially expensive" (Hays 1996, 8).

For international-adoptive mothers, appropriate culture keeping is an added responsibility of the "good mother." China-adoptive mothers, for example, reported being cognizant of their culture keeping being assessed by other adoptive parents and having to "keep up" with other China-adoptive families in their community. At the end of my visit with her, Nancy Thorne, a single mother with an eight-year-old daughter from China, for example, joked in an exasperated voice that recently the leaders in her FCC community had begun to take "roots tours" back to China with their children. These heritage tours, often running into thousands of dollars per family, take adoptees and their families back to the country of origin for sightseeing and cultural connection. Although Nancy wondered how she might logistically and financially pull it off, she imagined that she would be considered "out of step" if her family did not take such a trip. Nancy's comment reflects that the standard for China-adoptive culture keeping changes as new services, practices, or goods are added to the repertoire.

By engaging in correct levels of culture keeping—or at least by not being on the fringes—adoptive mothers, according to this perspective, not only fulfill their "duties" to their children but enable themselves to be assessed as "good" mothers. This was terribly important to the women I interviewed. They would ask me whether or not I thought they were doing enough (or doing too much) in terms of culture keeping. They wanted me to compare their culture keeping to others I had interviewed and assure them that they were performing up to par. This was an emotional issue for them. During one such exchange, a China-adoptive mother began to cry as she told me, "I just want to make sure I am doing it right—that I am doing it right for [my daughter]. I love her so much." In this exchange, we can see how symbolically meaningful proper culture keeping is to mothers' assessments of "good mothering" and to displays of affection for their children.

There was a small subset of women in the study—most prominent among Russia-adoptive mothers—who were vocal about the bind of intensive mothering. They spoke of the multiple and intense daily pressures they experienced in caring for their children, themselves, their careers, their husbands or partners, and their parents. One of the ways they responded to these pressures was by placing culture keeping on the back burner in order to attend to the many other items needing attention. One such mother, Emma Moore, found the demands of single parenting, her daughter's developmental health issues, and a professional job leaving little time for Russian culture keeping. Although apologetic at first, she stated, "I have a list of priorities that are more important [than Russian culture]." Rather than cast themselves as "bad mothers," these women defensively attempted to reframe their lack of deep engagement with culture keeping from an indication of inappropriate mothering to a consequence of fulfilling other important mothering demands.

Women's ability to know and engage in the correct level of culture keeping is one of the ways they assess themselves as mothers. This can be seen in the ways they were highly critical of adoptive mothers who participate in culture keeping at the extremes—both those who "go overboard" and those who choose to hide or ignore adopted children's ethnic and national origins by disregarding culture.

In contrast to the criticism they sometimes leveled against others, most of the women self-assessed their own culture keeping as "somewhere in the middle" of this culture keeping spectrum. The standards used for these self-assessments, however, differed quite dramatically between those with children from China and those with children from Russia. China-adoptive mothers referenced each other, while the Russia-adoptive mothers' reference group was a vague and amorphous adoption community. The China-adoptive mothers were much more familiar with the cultural practices of other families with children from the same country than the Russia-adoptive mothers. Because of this, the boundaries of culture keeping (and therefore, that which was considered normal or standard culture keeping) were much clearer within the China-adoptive group than in the Russia-adoptive group. In these differences, we can see important variations in the China- and Russia-adoptive communities and parenting experiences.

For China-adoptive mothers, culture keeping included membership or participation in FCC, contact with the group with whom families traveled to China, celebration of Chinese holidays (especially Chinese New Year), incorporating Chinese goods and foods into the home, involvement or volunteering with China adoptees' schools regarding cultural issues and lessons, talking about China positively with their children, formal Chinese study (e.g., language, dance, or culture), participating in culture camps and roots or heritage tours, and engagement with the Chinese community.

The China-adoptive mothers who spoke with me didn't always personally subscribe to this culture keeping model in full, yet nearly all the women understood it to be the normative standard for keeping culture, against which they judged their own efforts.

The reference group from which this culture keeping model grew and against which China-adoptive mothers assessed their own culture keeping was other China-adoptive families— either people personally known to them or people whom parents read about in newsletters or communicated with via China adoption internet groups or blogs. China-adoptive mothers described the culture keeping of friends or acquaintances in FCC, in their travel groups, in their local communities, and at their children's schools. They purported to know who was doing what and professed to understand why.

This well-known standard of culture keeping among China adopters contrasts with Russia-adoptive mothers for whom there was not a widely understood appropriate model for culture keeping. Compared to China-adoptive mothers, those with children from Russia less confidently assessed the culture keeping of others with children from the same country. They had far less contact with other parents who had adopted from the same country than did the China-adoptive group. Reflective of this difference, Russia-adoptive mothers rarely referenced other actual Russia-adoptive families in appraising their own participation with Russian culture. Rather, they judged themselves against the two extreme poles of culture keeping: total immersion or total Americanization.

The examples of "total immersion" Russia-adoptive

mothers shared with me were not of other families who had adopted from Russia but rather those with Asian children. Gwen McPhee, for example, was baffled by the "extreme" culture keeping of friends with children from Korea. She thought her friends were "obsessed" with Korean culture keeping because "they've gone to the Korean church" and "they went and learned Korean." Gwen was most bewildered by the fact that her friends "completely" changed the decor of their house to a Korean-style theme. She thought a more appropriate approach would have been to limit the Korean decorations to the child's room.

For many Russia-adoptive families, activities such as those engaged in by Gwen's friend (interacting with the ethnic community, language learning, and ethnic home decor) were viewed as part of an "obsession" with the birth culture. This contrasts with China-adoptive families for whom all of those activities constitute normal and normative culture keeping practices. I do not mean to imply that China-adoptive mothers do not also have specific views on cultural "obsession." All the adoptive mothers I interviewed have definite ideas about "going overboard" with culture. Yet only Russia-adoptive mothers regularly referenced extreme culture keepers when self-assessing their own practices.

One the other side of the spectrum, the "total Americanization" extreme discussed by Russia-adoptive mothers saw families who were, as Emma Moore summarized, "not aware, not dealing with it at all, my kid's American." Christina Denison spoke of the "total Americanization" extreme as a supplanting of the child's ethnicity with that of the parents, "where people were saying, 'My child is American and I'm Irish, so my child is Irish.'" Russia-adoptive mothers had clear ideas about what "total Americanization" would look like, but when pressed if they actually knew families who subscribed to this perspective, they gave noncommittal, vague replies, such as Gwen McPhee's response: "We traveled with some people that I think maybe, you know, might forget once they got home. But no, I don't [know anyone on that end of the spectrum]. You get that impression that once they got home with the kid, it was going to be a past memory. But that's just my impression."

With these two negative examples (i.e., "total immersion" and "total Americanization") as their reference points, none of the Russia-adoptive mothers actually assessed their own culture keeping at either extreme. As with China-adoptive mothers, women with children from Russia also reported themselves to be "somewhere in the middle" of the culture keeping spectrum. However, because Russia-adoptive mothers did not share a common culture keeping standard, the range of self-assessed "average" Russia culture keeping was much broader and included women who planned to go on "roots tours" *and* women whose only connection to Russia was in exchanges with the Russian pizza delivery man.

Because of the loose boundaries of Russia culture keeping, there was a great deal more variation in the cultural orientation and participation of Russia-adoptive mothers than among China-adoptive ones. China culture keeping was simply institutionalized in ways absent among the Russia-adoption community. This speaks to differences in parental socialization and group cohesion between the China- and Russia-adoptive communities.

In the balancing act between inclusion and difference, we can see the multiple constraints faced by international-adoptive mothers as they attempt to structure culture keeping into their families' lives. Among both groups, there was a widespread understanding that adoptive parents *should* attempt to keep culture. Deliberately discouraging one's child from making connections to his or her birth culture was seen as taboo and, therefore, no one self-assessed themselves as engaging in such behavior.

Even mothers who did not (or could not) incorporate ethnic practices into their families' lives espoused a philosophical commitment to culture keeping. This was especially prevalent among Russia adopters. While two-thirds of the women with children from Russia in my sample *told me* that culture keeping was important, an equal number *did not engage* with Russian culture beyond a thinly applied, superficial level.

This contradiction between professed belief and actual practice points to the fact that although culture keeping is posed by professionals as the antidote to challenges that arise from living as an internationally adoptive family, culture keeping itself poses various dilemmas for mothers. While they overwhelmingly ascribe to a philosophical commitment to culture keeping as necessary for healthy childhood self-esteem, they also hold the (often conflicting) desire to facilitate inclusion of their child in their surrounding social milieu. They are afraid of both "going overboard" with culture and fearful that they won't do enough. If they are unable or unwilling to engage in culture keeping, some (especially Russia-adoptive mothers) defensively report the plethora of mothering demands that keep them from doing so. Or they argue that they are protecting their children from stigma. They believe others will criticize them if they do not engage in appropriate levels of culture keeping—that they will not be seen as good adoptive mothers—yet they believe their children will reject their culture keeping efforts (and maybe reject them as parents also) if they push culture too much.

It is in negotiating these various constraints that mothers attempt to bridge the gap between the ideological "American Family" and their actual lived experience in international-adoptive families. That negotiation centers, therefore, on normalizing family difference.

Normalizing Difference in China-Adoptive Families

> The kids know they're Chinese; we celebrate some of the
> big Chinese holidays that we know of; I'm sure we screw
> up half the traditions. So we do what we can, but it's kind
> of—I don't want to ram it down their throats either, to
> distinguish them so much from the rest of our family.
> —Shannon Lynch, China-adoptive mother

China-adoptive mothers center their efforts on the normalization of the racial make-up of their families. This evidenced itself in the ways women spoke of inclusion and difference in terms of the multiple racial or national identities within their families. Most women equated an American identity with "being the same" (i.e., being white) and a Chinese identity with "being different" (i.e., being foreign). American-ness is characterized in the interview narratives as uncomplicated and relaxed—not needing to be thought about or worked over. It is about connection and sameness and is represented by images of relaxed freedom for children. In contrast, Chinese-ness (especially what mothers would call "real" Chinese—food, holidays, clothes, country, or people) requires thought and labor; it is complicated and takes mothers outside of their usual comfort zones.

These identities, as described by China-adoptive mothers, are both about who people are (their primordial or achieved identities) and what they do (the activities in which they engage). Using this rubric, mothers spoke of "American kids" as those who participate in "normal things": certain types of activities, most especially activities that are not "ethnic," that are not Chinese; activities that emphasize their normalcy. Against that image, mothers pose their own children. Their children, they argue, are American, yet they are racialized as "Chinese," as "racialized Other" (than white).

It was primarily this balance between "American" (coded as same-ness and located in the ascribed identity of the parents and the achieved identity of the child) and "Chinese" (coded as other, as different, and located in the ascribed identity of the child) that China-adoptive mothers sought to balance. Mothers wanted their children to have interests outside of Chinese ones and have the time to enjoy them. Nancy Thorne's sentiment that she didn't want Chinese culture to preclude her daughter's involvement "in other things that she wants to do as just a kid" was common. According to this logic, to be "just a kid" was to not be engaging in Chinese-related activities. It was important, Nancy argued, for children to have time for "just being an American kid, skinning their knees as they ride through the neighborhood." Against the backdrop of foreign Chinese ethnicity, other activities ("skinning their knees" as they ride their bikes) were cast as distinctly "American." "Chinese-ness" was framed by mothers as a set of practices and an identity that contrasts with the normalized "American" identity. To be Chinese, therefore, and to engage in Chinese activities, differentiates oneself from being American.

This perspective is not unique to adoptive parents. Others have noted this American/foreign divide regarding the way in which Asian Americans are situated in the dominant U.S. racial schema (see Kibria 2002a; Tuan 1998). In her study on the Asian American ethnic experience, Mia Tuan notes, "Ultimately, being an American is equated with being white" (1998, 40). It is precisely the racial otherness, the Chinese-ness, of their children, mothers argued, that makes their children unique or different and sets them apart from those (white) Americans around them.

Ironically, by bifurcating "Chinese" and "American" activities (and children), most women were not allowing room for the actual space their children will fill: Chinese American. There is no place in their American/Chinese divide for the cultural activities of Chinese Americans. One is either white/ American or Asian/foreign. The mechanism through which China-adoptive mothers managed these two contrasting racialized identities was "culture." Other researchers have noted how "culture" operates as a proxy for race among white mothers with adopted Asian children (see Anagnost 2000; Dorow 2006a; Moosenick 2004). Nora Rose Moosenick, for example, noted that for mothers of Korean children, "Culture, not race was their focus. The suggestion was made that culture, not race distinguished these women from their children. These women worked to provide their children a culturally sensitive upbringing emphasizing Korean culture, but they talked about doing so, most often, without overtures to race" (2004, 126).

Perhaps given the increased emphasis on the acknowledgment of difference, and the particularly cohesive nature of the China-adoptive community, many women in my sample spoke more directly about race than did those in Moosenick's study. Like Moosenick's sample, however, it was culture that the adoptive mothers in my study emphasized in terms of the mechanism used to address difference. Although women used the language of "cultural difference," it *was* race they were attempting to address. It was the racial difference of their children (from other "Americans," i.e., whites) that China-adoptive mothers attempted to manage through the amount of culture keeping in which they engaged. In other words, mothers sought to negotiate inclusion and difference through engagement with Chinese culture. Culture keeping, therefore, was as much about becoming American as it was about facilitating a Chinese identity. This balancing act was challenging. Vivian Lutz characterized it as a "real tension between wanting to pick them out and say you're different, you're special, you need to go to Chinese school versus, you know, you can do things that everybody else seems to be doing."

The "everyone else" Vivian is referring to is a generalized non-Chinese (white) American. In their decisions on how to engage in culture keeping, China-adoptive mothers were attempting to address the racial difference between their children and "everyone else."

However, it is not only their children's racial difference (to their adoptive families and others in their communities) that mothers manage through culture keeping, it is *their own racial difference* to Chinese. For the majority of China-adoptive mothers, culture keeping takes them outside of their familiar routines, communities, and experiences. Most mothers shared that they rarely had even thought about China and never sought out news from that country before they adopted their children. Prior to bringing her first daughter home from China, Eloise Nolan said, "I didn't really think much about China before. You know, you hear it in the news and just blow it off. And now when you hear anything about China it's like, *Oh, what's going on?* Now I really hone in on it."

Post-adoption, mothers felt hyper-aware when news from China surfaced. China had become a part of their lives and they strived for it to be integrated naturally; however, their own social and cultural distance from China made this difficult. While some women had spent time in China (prior to beginning the adoption process) or studied Chinese language or arts in college, most had not. For the majority of women, adopting their children was their first foray into integrating China into their lives. Moreover, even those who characterized themselves as having long-time interests in China had to educate themselves on China and Chinese customs in order to enact the type of Chinese culture they engaged in with their children. As Leanne Becker told me, "It feels like I have to study so hard to learn how to celebrate the holidays in our home."

These efforts brought new feelings of connectedness to China for mothers. Mothering their Chinese children, they reported, brought a richness to their lives that had not been present before. It made them "passionate about learning about Asia." They genuinely enjoyed this aspect of their families. Stacey Dita shared, "It feels like it sort of added this whole element and dimension to my life that is, you know, I explain to people when they say, 'Why did you adopt from another country?' The positives for me, the huge positives, are to bring this culture into our home. I mean, if you look upstairs my entire library upstairs is reading about China. There are a lot of books coming out now about the Cultural Revolution, people's experience growing up, I mean I love these books and I've gotten myself very immersed in this culture which is so fascinating."

Mothers felt a deep connection to the country of China, its culture, and its people. They tried to convey their love of China to their daughters through culture keeping. China-adoptive mothers reported an appreciation for the rich history of China and the beauty of Chinese music, art, and people. This was, however, a deeply felt connection to an amorphous "Chinese people," mostly those "over there" in China (i.e., "real Chinese") and not to actual people in their lives. It did not translate into actual friendships or deep meaningful day-to-day relationships with Chinese people here in the United States. For example, without referencing actual individuals, Carey Armstrong characterized her connection as an "affinity towards Chinese people" that she didn't have before. Most mothers reported this China connection without it having changed their actual racial or ethnic networks of friends or acquaintances. For example, although Shirley McIntosh had no Chinese or Asian American friends, she dubbed herself a "Chinese patriot" who "hated to hear anything bad" said about China.

Most women reported a more complicated relationship to China vis-à-vis the political and social situation. However, they all struggled with how to share the political reality of China and their child's abandonment stories with their daughters in ways that would not lead their children to have negative feelings about China or themselves. The most popular strategy used was to give a decidedly positive spin to all aspects of China and Chinese culture for their children. Perhaps because of this scrubbed-up positive spin on all things Chinese, learning about China and engaging in a Chinese cultural education for their children profoundly enriched but did not politically complicate their lives.

While mothers derived a great deal of pleasure bringing Chinese ethnicity into their homes, they were also self-conscious about their efforts to keep culture. They enjoyed learning about the positive aspects of China and sharing them with their children, yet it was "constant work" to "figure out organic ways" of keeping culture. Many mothers were critical about their culture keeping strategies and characterized their efforts as lacking and inauthentic. Leanne Becker joked that it felt like "white women playing Chinese." Vivian Lutz described culture keeping by adoptive parents as "white parents teaching their children" an "imagined view of Chinese culture," which "profoundly unsettled" her. These women struggled with incorporating Chinese culture into the flow of their daily lives in ways that made them comfortable.

And this was the challenge: what they viewed as "authentic" forms of Chinese culture (represented most readily by engagement with the Chinese diaspora) felt inauthentic for them to be engaging in because they themselves were not Chinese. Lorraine Burg, for example, characterized her initial attempts to bring Chinese culture into her daughter's life, which included trips to Chinatown and attendance at events sponsored by the Chinese community, as "just dumb" because it was "just sort of an exercise, it [was] not really real."

To be "really real," they needed to engage in culture keeping that was authentic in two different ways: authentic in that it was authentically Chinese culture, and authentic in that they felt authentic when engaging in it. These women desired to move effortlessly between their immediate social world (largely white) and their intentionally created Chinese world. Their ideal was to blend these two worlds into an authentic day-to-day family life.

"Authentic culture," however, was challenging. There was an understanding among my sample that their Chinese cultural practices would be (and are) viewed by others as inauthentic and incorrect. While some have been critical of the naiveté in which adoptive parents engage in commodified and superficial culture (see Anagnost 2000), many women in my study were aware and concerned about the artificiality of their cultural practices. Some women did attempt to find more genuine forms of Chinese culture to practice. Lorraine Burg's statement, "I'm always trying to find ways to bring culture—Chinese culture —into our home that does not feel completely artificial," was echoed by many other participants. In part, it was the "constant work" of having to think about and plan how to do Chinese culture keeping that made mothers self-conscious and made their practices feel artificial.

Part of this self-consciousness surrounding culture keeping stemmed from the relationship international-adoptive families have with the Chinese ethnic community. Mothers saw their interactions with Chinese adults and families as a wonderful medium for keeping culture for their children. They thought it was important for their daughters to have interactions with other Chinese people in order to realize that, as Charlotte Gordon said, being adopted is "not the only way to be Chinese."

China-adoptive mothers were very specific about which Chinese community they wished to embrace. Most women wanted to forge connections in the Chinese *immigrant* community rather than with later-generation *Chinese Americans.* They saw immigrants as practicing a more genuine Chinese culture and accessing more authentic forms of "Chinese-ness." They did not want a "watered-down version" of Chinese-ness and, largely, did not appear interested in Chinese American history or politics. They wanted to tap into Chinese, not Chinese American, culture.

Ironically, this struggle with authenticity, which China-adoptive mothers perceived to be unique to international adoption, can actually be found among Asian immigrants and Asian Americans themselves (see Kibria 2002a; Louie 2002; Louie 2008; Zhou 2000). Struggles over "authenticity," over adaptation (or assimilation) to American culture, over upholding tradition, over acculturation to the host culture, and over enculturation to the "ethnic family" culture are common among immigrant populations, especially among later-generation ethnic-minority youth. This is true of the very "authentic" population that China-adoptive mothers are seeking. In her work among immigrant families in New York's Chinatown, Min Zhou writes, "While assimilation is the ultimate goal for the Chinese American family, parents are constantly caught in the conflict between maintenance of cultural identity in children and the adoption of desirable mainstream cultural ways" (2000, 325).

These cultural struggles of the Chinese immigrant and later-generation population appear to be invisible to the China-adoptive mothers with whom I spoke. Rather, adoptive mothers relied upon static notions of traditional, authentic culture residing primordially in the "ethnic" body.

They wanted access to that authentic culture for their children. But while they declared the Chinese community to be welcoming, hardly any attempts had been made to integrate deeply into that world. I see the character of interethnic relations in New England, historically strained, as helping to shape this disconnect.[2] Few mothers reported that they had close intimate relationships with Chinese adults. Rather, their points

of contact were with Chinese adults engaged (para)-profession-
ally in services to the Chinese adoption community (such as
language or dance classes for the Chinese adoptee). While several mothers were on friendly terms with these (para)profes-
sionals, only two participants with children from China cited
an Asian person as a friend.

For most women, their main contact with Chinese adults,
outside of (paid) instructors, was with strangers in public settings: at restaurants, festivals, grocery stores, Chinatown, or as
presenters or guests at adoption group events.

Some mothers were utilitarian in their interactions with
Chinese strangers. They sought out Chinese ethnics as cultural
experts in the hopes of garnering specific skills or knowledge in
order to better keep culture for their children. Unless the interaction occurred in a venue specific to cultural exchange, such
as a cultural fair or adoption group event, these interactions
were usually unsatisfactory for adoptive mothers. Charlotte
Gordon spoke of how her need to gather cultural information
from Chinese adults dominated her interactions with them:

> I want more things from them. I want to ask them all to be a
> resource for me [*laughter*]; which isn't really very fair. I tend
> to want information much quicker. It's like, "Hello. Nice to
> meet you. Do you know where I can do this?" [*laughter*]

While Charlotte noted that forcing others to be the cultural
experts for their ethnic group "isn't really fair," she seemed
relatively comfortable with this approach. In addition to these
utilitarian exchanges, most women wanted to bring more Chinese people into their day-to-day lives. While many mothers
saw Asian faces (other than those of their children) regularly,
few spoke of having interactions that could lead to more meaningful relationships. Although they stated a desire to have

deeper connections in the ethnic community, they did little to see this come to fruition. There was a barrier to intimacy that the mothers had a hard time scaling.

The difficulties mothers faced connecting to Chinese adults speaks to the racially segregated lives the families in this study lead, as do many in the United States (Massey and Denton 1993). Because of this, in seeking out Chinese strangers in public, some mothers reveal a naiveté regarding contemporary race relations. Shirley McIntosh, for example, makes an "assumption of foreignness" (Tuan 1998) that anyone Asian is Chinese and that anyone Chinese is a Chinese immigrant and not American. She displayed this when she told me,

> Every time I see someone who looks Chinese, I say, "Are you Chinese?" Everywhere I go, "Are you Chinese? You from China? My baby is from China." They're like, "Okay, she's a freak." [*laughter*] Oh yeah, absolutely. I had some people who were interested in buying my car recently. It was like, "Are you Chinese? Are you from China?" I get into this conversation, "Well, let me show you pictures of my baby." Yeah, so it's been fun.

This type of interaction, while "fun" for Shirley and other adoptive mothers with children from China, helps to sustain the racial marginalization of Asian Americans. Part of the problem is that these women live in largely white middle-class worlds and have difficulty meeting large numbers of Chinese Americans or Chinese immigrants in what they consider "natural" settings. While mothers might have Asian co-workers or neighbors they interact with regularly, for the most part they did not have intimate connections with Asians. Although everyone knew where to find large numbers of Chinese immigrants (e.g., Chinatowns, at Chinese businesses and events, and Chinese community centers), most did not feel they knew a way to engage with them.

Some mothers worried about how the politics of Chinese international adoption would play out in interactions with Chinese adults. This worried Nancy Thorne, who shared, "I often wonder, you know, if we're in Chinatown or somewhere where there are a lot of Chinese Americans, how they would think about me taking one of their children out of their country." (Note how Nancy refers to being unsure how Chinese *Americans*—whose country is the United States—would feel about her taking a child out of "their country" [i.e., China]. This is a good example of how Chinese Americans are not seen as true Americans but rather associated with their country of ancestral origin.) Rachel Abramson spoke about the guilt she feels for "taking these girls out of China" and stated that she is "always amazed that Chinese were not more appalled of how we come there with our wealth and steal their daughters." This guilt keeps some mothers from attempting to forge relationships with Chinese people or even attempting casual interactions.

It was not only a sensitivity over the issue of international adoption, however, that made mothers self-conscious and impeded contact with Chinese people. It was also the racial and cultural difference *they themselves* experienced in Chinese settings. Women did venture to Chinatown with the goal of exposing their daughters to Chinese culture and connecting with Chinese people. However, they largely reported being self-conscious and awkward in Chinatown because of what that meant for them racially (being in the racial minority in Chinatown) and culturally (being unable to understand both the language and the interactions of the neighborhood or community). Lynn Werden lamented, "You know, I wish I were more culturally facile myself. Like I could learn to speak Chinese or I was somebody who would never be awkward when I go to Chinatown. It's like, 'I have no idea what is going on!' "

These women were accustomed to having more understanding and control in social and institutional settings than was available to them in Chinatown. While they still ventured into Chinese dominated spaces, owing to these difficulties in interethnic relations, they tended to have rather superficial relationships with Chinese ethnics.

In making their decisions on how to engage in Chinese culture keeping, China-adoptive mothers sought to balance their children's racial difference from whites and their own racial and cultural difference from Chinese. Because of this, they largely keep culture by concentrating their most involved efforts on consumerism and by engaging with other white adoptive families with children from China, largely through the organization Families with Children from China (FCC).

FCC is a national organization run by parent volunteers. Regional and local chapters organize "newsletters, membership directories, family picnics and potluck suppers, celebrations of Chinese festivals and holidays, pre-adoption information meetings, playgroups, Chinese language and culture classes for children, and parent speakers" (*fwcc.org*). FCC New England has an online newsletter and electronic mailing list (*fccne.org*). FCC is an important purveyor of Chinese cultural information and events in New England.

Although it is difficult to determine how prevalent FCC membership is among all China-adoptive families in the United States, the women in my study reported membership in FCC as virtually obligatory. In and of itself, however, FCC membership did not necessarily translate into high FCC participation, nor did it mean that women were uncritical of the group. However, FCC membership and all that it entailed was seen as one of the standard mechanisms for performing culture keeping obligations.

Participants in my study reported that actual participation in FCC waxes and wanes depending upon the stage of adoption (pre-adoptive parents are welcome at FCC events and meetings), the age of the children, the amount of time since the adoption (people with younger children and those who had recently adopted reported higher levels of participation), and the event (FCC Chinese New Year parties were popular). However, membership in FCC was talked about by the women in my study as a natural and inevitable part of being a China-adoptive mother.[3]

Many women and their children also participated in smaller groups for China-adoptive families, such as those that grew out of formal Chinese language or culture classes, or more loosely organized play groups or friendship circles. The most common source of these smaller groups was the "adoption travel group" (the group of families with whom one travels to collect the child). While not all travel groups stay connected, many women spoke of annual reunions where parents and children spend time together. Often these get-togethers involve overnight or long weekend stays at a member's home or family friendly vacation spot. The mothers who were members of active travel groups enjoyed their involvement. Again, membership in groups that were active was reported to be essentially obligatory; as Jacqueline Sorokin attests, "Everybody goes because *this is what you do*" [emphasis in original].

Being active in one's travel group was seen as an indicator of one's commitment to culture keeping—in effect, as a barometer of being a "good" China-adoptive mom. Cautionary tales of travel group members that disconnected themselves from their groups highlight how women equated travel group participation with "good adoptive mothering." Apostates were criticized by participants as anti-Chinese, anti-social, and strong American patriots determined to raise their children without "Chinese" influences.

China adoption groups perform a significant role in the lives of China adopters. The most important aspect of membership in adoption groups was the access it gave families to each other. Most significantly, women reported, the adopted children were able to socialize with other Chinese adoptees at group get-togethers and events. Many internationally adopted children live in largely white worlds, and these groups, participating mothers argued, are important because they allow their children opportunities to experience the feeling of being in the racial majority (if even for a couple of hours). Leanne Becker spoke of how, at FCC events, China adoptees "can be in environments where almost all the kids are Chinese; where almost everybody looks like them. A sea of three hundred Chinese faces, which I think is great for them. I think it's really empowering for them to be able to feel like all the white kids in the class feel every day of the week."

In addition to the benefits of (rather fleetingly) being in the statistical racial majority, mothers also looked to the groups as a source of long-term friends for their children. They wanted their children to develop deep friendships with other Chinese kids being raised by white parents in adoptive homes. Many adoptive mothers found this aspect of group membership invaluable. By developing a friendship base with other young Chinese adoptees, mothers hoped that their children felt "a sense of belonging and importance" otherwise lacking in their daily lives.

Mothers were keenly committed to the idea that their children not feel as if they were the only adopted Chinese child with white parents, but that they had a large group of friends who were as well. They found this especially important as they looked ahead to their child's adolescence. Many women voiced concerns over the alienation (and resulting family discord) they fear their children will experience due to racial, ethnic, and adoptive minority status. Adoption groups, and the friendships that arise from them, were seen as a protective shield that could buffer their children against that alienation. Mothers anticipated that these friendships would operate as a social support network and pressure valve for their children during troublesome teenage years.

These women also looked to these groups for friendships for themselves. Having the support and camaraderie of other white adoptive moms with girls from China was vitally important to participants. Rachel Abramson joked about attending her group: "If my daughter doesn't feel like coming, I say, you're coming, absolutely, she has no choice, I'm coming!" These women felt a sense of connection with other adoptive mothers in these groups that they did not experience with parents of biologically born children. Stacey Dita said, "Certainly when I brought my daughter home I wasn't going to join a parenting group where people are talking about breastfeeding and delivery and things like that!"

These groups allowed mothers the opportunities to exchange information, ask questions, and offer support and advice on general parenting issues but, most important, on issues related to adoption, ethnicity, and race. Mothers turned to their friends as sounding boards (and advice panels) when their children were experiencing something problematic to see if the particular issue was adoption- or race-related.

The connections made in these groups came to be thought of and experienced by many as a type of kinship. Parents often referred to the kids in these groups as "cousins" or "sisters." Jacqueline Sorokin said, about her travel group, "I know there are people in this group for whom another member or other members have become their primary support, the closest friends, almost like sisters, cousins. We call them, the girls get together and we call them the cousins because that's what they're like."

Mothers use the language of biological kinship when talking about their daughters' relationships to each other. As one woman argued, the adoption travel group is the children's "connection, all their roots."

Mothers not only spoke of the adoptees as (fictive) kin but in practice, for many, these groups function as fictive "families." Many spend free time together, call each other for advice, take trips together, swap childcare, help each other when family members are ill, and attend each others family celebrations. It is the experience of adoption that brings these families together. However it is the children's shared origins—of ethnicity, region, or orphanage—that cements these friendships and produces a "fictive kinship" (Stack 1974).

However, at the same time that participants were arguing a de facto kinship between the children and an inherent connection amongst families, the mothers were quick to frame their friendships with each other as genuine and not solely rooted in shared experience or ethnicity. It was important to them that their friendships with other China-adoptive families be understood as legitimate, not forced or orchestrated. When describing these friendships mothers emphasized that they "really did like" each other. As Nancy Thorne explained when discussing her friendship with another family from her travel group, "They're just our friends and they happen to have an adopted child." These groups function as de facto family in which membership is intentionally chosen and other members well-liked.

By primarily locating culture keeping within the China-adoptive community, mothers found an enjoyable and supportive strategy for engaging with Chinese culture. These connections were explicitly about relationships with other interracial adoptive families with children from China and not about connections to children (or adults) in the Chinese ethnic community. Lorraine Burg elaborated:

I think that it's really important to know other people who have the same experience, which is having adopted kids from China. And then you kind of experience your Chinese culture through your own lives and your own experience because that's all it's ever, that's the only way it is ever going to make sense anyway. I mean Pearl is only going to experience it through who she is, which is, she has a white mother and she was adopted from China. She doesn't have a Chinese mom, she doesn't have a Chinese grandmother, she doesn't have those things. So, and to pretend like she does or to play act that she does, I think is unhealthy. So, I guess the primary thing would be to have relationships with people who have the same experience as we have.

Like Lorraine, many China-adoptive mothers want to facilitate an authentically *experienced* Chinese culture for their children, one that honestly reflects the makeup of their families, even if that means forgoing what they characterize as more genuine forms of Chinese culture. By keeping culture through the adoption community, these women are able to ensure that their children experienced other families like their own.

In this strategy, they balance difference for their daughters *and* for themselves. While some women seem genuinely to believe that the cultural lessons learned and consumer goods purchased through China-adoptive culture were "authentically Chinese," most understood that they were merely an approximation. Lorraine, for example, spoke of the cultural practices of adoptive families as "not really Chinese culture" but rather "FCC culture." While some women were uncomfortable with the inauthentic nature of the Chinese culture in which they were engaged, they found it to be a deeply pleasurable way to fulfill the call to socialize their children ethnically. Part of this pleasure was located in the consumptive nature of much of China culture keeping. They also derived support from the friendships they developed with other China-adoptive families. They felt as though they were attentive to racial issues as they were providing their children with Chinese friends—"cousins," even. While they viewed this type of culture keeping as not entirely authentic to China, it was authentic to their experiences as interracial China-adoptive families. In this way, mothers attempt to normalize family differences in white/Asian China-adoptive families.

Normalizing Difference in Russia-Adoptive Families

> I just kind of raise my children and feel comfortable with that. And almost, you know, it flips between wanting to do the right thing [and keep Russian culture] and wanting to just feel that they are yours. You know, and get that other piece a little more in the background. How important is it on a *daily basis?* Let's just be a family.
>
> —Roberta Palmer, Russia-adoptive mother

Mothers with children from Russia also seek to balance various identities for their children through the ways in which they engage in culture keeping. Unlike white China-adoptive mothers, however, those with children from Russia do not need to address interraciality within their monoracial families. The difference they seek to normalize for their children is both ethnic and non-biological kinship. The strategies they use to address ethnic difference (i.e., between "Russian-ness" versus "American-ness") within their families vary more widely than the approaches used by China-adoptive mothers.

A minority of women with children from Russia engaged seriously in culture keeping. For these women, their children's "Russian-ness" was not posed as a status that would preclude or overshadow their American identities—although Russia and America were distinct from one another. This contrasts with the narratives of bifurcation connected to birth culture identity in China-adoptive mothers' narratives. Culture keeping Russia-adoptive families expressed multicultural identities. Not only were their families multicultural, in that they honored the ethnicities of both child and parent, but the child herself was seen to be multicultural, having both Russian *and* American identities. These dual identities tempered the amount of Russian culture keeping in which families participated. For example, Christina Denison characterized her daughter as "an American from Russia" who, therefore, was not going to be enrolled in Russian courses or exposed to the "total immersion" method of language and culture education.

While these mothers saw Russian-ness as an intrinsic part of their child's identity, they strove for what they saw as the correct balance between being Russian and being American. They did not, however, question their children's American status or doubt their ability to be accepted in white America. They were concerned, however, that over-emphasizing their Russian heritage might create difficulties for their children as white, middle-class American children. Carol Acher stated that, although she wants to be "very open" about Russian culture with her daughter, overt displays are not part of her strategy. She wants her daughter "to always be able to ask questions, but we're not going to hang a Russian flag out in front of our home either . . . We don't want her to be something that could make her different. We want it to be part of who she is and who we are as a family and something that adds to the whole."

While these women were the most highly engaged in culture keeping among my sample of mothers with children from Russia, Carol's concern that her family's engagement with Russian culture not in any way make her daughter feel "different" from other children was a common apprehension. These women were preemptive about confronting the stigma of non-biological kinship and ethnic difference. While they were interested in keeping their children exposed to Russian culture, they were equally—if not more—concerned about "shoving" culture down their children's throats. Therefore, while the mothers valued the Russian origins of their children, it was not integrated into the day-to-day lives of their families to any great extent. They sometimes participated in cultural activities, maintained friendships with one or two other adoptive families with children from Russia, attended FRUA events, and occasionally ate Russian food, but as Kerry summed up when asked what it meant to her that her daughter was Russian,

> I don't think it much matters, really, in a way. Being a parent is being a parent. I don't really think that on a day to day basis it makes a huge difference. I'm not sure how to answer that. [*laughter*] I mean, not that we don't value where she's from; it's just that it's not something that really—that affects any of our relationship . . . it matters, but it doesn't matter, you know?

The vehicle that allowed Russia-adoptive mothers (but not China-adoptive ones) to ensure that ethnicity "matters, but it doesn't matter," that their children "were not something that could make them different" was, of course, the majority white racial status shared by children and parents. For most Russia-adoptive families, this racial similarity between parent and child was strongly emphasized with culture keeping playing a minimal role in their lives.

While a minority of Russia-adoptive mothers integrated Russian culture alongside parental heritage, the majority of families had sporadic contact with other Russia-adoptive families and only superficial integration of Russian culture, often centering on the Christmas holiday. Russian ethnicity was safely contained in shallow sporadic interactions and private celebrations.

For these families, cultural difference (between "Russian" and "American") was flattened and racial similarity (whiteness) was heightened. These mothers spoke of whiteness as a dynamic identity that allows for children and parents to bond. Brenda Cole said, of her son, "Marko blends right in. No one can project on him that he's from another culture. I think probably if kids have, you know, present as being from another culture then there is an expectation that they're familiar with that culture." The fact that Russian-born children can racially blend with their adoptive U.S. families and in their white communities is unique among internationally adoptive families, the majority of whom, as detailed in earlier chapters, are interracial. Dotty Cohen remarked upon this when she spoke about the differences between adopting from Russia and from China:

> Well, I think that probably the difference between Russia and China is, if you are adopting from Russia, likely, you are adopting a Caucasian child. The notion that that child comes from another culture isn't in society's face. So it doesn't necessarily reflect back on the child. I think that's really different than when you do transcultural adoption. When you deal with transcultural adoption, there's another identity issue. There's another layer of identity that the child has to really deal with. Some of the ways that's played out is by bringing the culture into the family.

Dotty and Brenda's comments illuminate the general approach to race and culture among those Russia-adoptive mothers who do not engage deeply with birth culture. These women find culture keeping unnecessary within their families because their children are white and able to "blend in." Women who largely avoided birth culture also avoided directly naming race or the racial privileges their families experience. They talked around the issue, skirting race directly by talking about "transcultur-alism" and "physical identity." Notice that Dotty uses culture as a proxy for race: she calls trans*racial* adoptions trans*cultural* and in doing so equates (white) Americans adopting white children from Russia as mono*cultural,* which, in fact, is not the case. I see this as indicative of a deeper orientation to race, and not a mere linguistic slip.

Scholars of critical white theory argue that whiteness itself "occupies a hegemonic position precisely because it cannot and will not speak its own name" (Kenny 2000b, 114). Other researchers have noted an avoidance of naming race among their white research participants and have argued this is a particular response to the ways in which whiteness is privileged in the United States (Devault 1995; Frankenberg 1993; Kenny 2000a and 2000b; Twine 1997). They argue that the privileges of being white in a racially stratified society are so far-reaching, so taken for granted, and so enmeshed in our daily interactions that they appear to be not benefits, but a normal part of the "natural" order (Bush 2004; Frankenberg 1993; McKinney 2005; Wildman 1996). Matt Wray and Annalee Newitz call this "the unraced center of a racialized world" (1997, 3).

Part of white privilege enjoyed by middle- and upper-class whites is the element of choice in decisions regarding the expression of one's own ethnic life (Tuan 1998; Waters 1990). This feeling of belonging culturally, of being one of the majority with the power to control one's own life—specifically one's own and one's children's ethnic life—is a unique attribute of white middle-class families who are (or appear) biologically related to their children.[4]

White international-adoptive mothers have access to white racial privilege (even if they do not recognize it as such). Through their approach to culture keeping, we can see ways in which they attempt to construct the same privilege for their children. Part of the privilege experienced by those mothering white children is the ability to ignore, downplay, or celebrate ones ethnic heritage within one's family without fear, pressure, or social costs (Tuan 1998; Waters 1990). Unlike China-adoptive mothers, Russia-adoptive mothers contend that their children do not experience the expectation that they engage with Russian culture or possess knowledge about Russia. Nor do they need to practice their birth ethnicity, because of their ability to "blend in" racially. For these women, race is used to erase ethnic difference. It is specifically because of the children's racial status as whites and the fact that they share this privileged location with their parents that connections to and the practice of Russian culture are seen as unnecessary.

In this way, the ethnic practices of these families parallels the symbolic ethnicity of non-adoptive white families in the United States. Alba (1990, 205) found that U.S. white (non-adoptive) parents do little to encourage white ethnic identities in their children. He found that "only a minority of parents want their children to identify [ethnically], and an even smaller minority take forthright steps to encourage them to do so. If the identities of the next generation depend on the decisions and actions of contemporary parents, then ethnic identity will undergo a decline in the future, for parents are more likely to identify themselves than to want their children to do so."

The culture keeping approach of many Russia-adoptive mothers differs from symbolic ethnicity, however, in that many Russia-adoptive mothers understood even minimal engagement with culture to be problematic (although they still cast themselves as dedicated to culture and average culture keepers). Because of this, Russia-adoptive mothers had a much different relationship to Russia-adoption organizations such as Families for Russian and Ukrainian Adoption (FRUA) than did China-adoptive mothers.

FRUA, a national organization for those who have adopted from the countries of the former Soviet Union, circulates a quarterly newsletter and offers a website with message boards. The local FRUA New England chapter is one of the oldest chapters in the country, with approximately one hundred member families. According to its website (*www.frua newengland.org*), the FRUA New England chapter is a support group that "holds cultural, social and educational events for families, circulates a chapter newsletter and maintains orphanage relief charitable programs." It also holds an annual Russian-Ukrainian festival that includes Russian performers (a clown from the Moscow State Circus, for example), Russian goods for sale, and catered Russian food.

The majority of women with Russian children who spoke with me had actually held membership or had participated, at one time or another, in activities run by FRUA. However, membership in this group was not seen as obligatory, nor did it translate into access to the number of other families or organized activities that membership in FCC did for China-adoptive mothers.

Russia-adoptive mothers who participated in adoption groups such as FRUA did so for the opportunities they provided to meet other families for playdates at child-friendly locations, such as the zoo or local parks. These women also relied on FRUA to receive information about Russian cultural practices and to connect with other adoptive families. Some mothers chose to participate in only those FRUA events with cultural themes. Judy Inman shared, "FRUA really does events that are much more culturally targeted, which is the way I like FRUA." It was important, however, to others that FRUA events not be too heavily laden with a Russian cultural message but rather focus simply on the opportunity to interact with other families with children from Russia. These women wanted participation in FRUA to be normalized in their children's lives and not something that made them different from other children. These mothers framed participation with FRUA, therefore, as friendship-based rather than culture-based. Carol Acher spoke of the way Russian cultural connections were only subtly made through participation in FRUA: "Elana knows about FRUA. She knows it is other children born throughout Eastern Europe. But we don't highlight that. We say, *We're going to the zoo with the FRUA people.* And then we go and we have a great time. She's got friends that she's made. And then later on the drive home, we might say something about, *You know, you had such fun. Wasn't it nice to see Alexei and Simone and Nadia? It's so cool to be all born in Russia. You know I love that you all have that connection.* And that's the end of the discussion."

Because FRUA itself is a smaller organization with fewer members and events, several Russia-adoptive mothers spoke of feeling out of place at gatherings, especially if they were single parents. Some women turned instead to general adoption playgroups.[5] One of these women, Gwen McPhee, preferred her group that included "a mix of adoptive families from all situations" rather than only married couples with children from Eastern Europe. These adoption groups provided mothers the opportunity to give and receive support on general adoption related issues as well as parenting matters.

Interest in these groups also speaks to the idea that these women find friendships or connections for their children in the general adoption community as important as (or in replacement of) those they may have with other families with children from Russia. For example, for Gwen McPhee, the "common bond" she had with others in her playgroup centered on the fact that they were all adoptive mothers, not that they had all adopted from the same country. Adoption playgroups, whether organized through FRUA or more general organizations, were important for women in that they provided a space in which they were able to "let their guard down" with other mothers. Playgroups organized for adoptive families naturalize adoptive parenting. Rather than standing out as the only adoptive mothers among many biological ones, these groups afford members much-needed anonymity from biological scrutiny. In adoption playgroups, there are no uncomfortable moments of adoption disclosure. Having a "shared path" to parenting, as Carol Acher put it, affords members the experience of having one's family formation strategy normalized. It also gives members the opportunity to speak freely about specific adoption-related concerns or issues.

While the friendships derived from adoption groups (or with other adoptive mothers more generally) were important in the lives of several of these involved Russia-adoptive mothers, these were not especially cherished relationships for most. This was a stark contrast to the experiences of China-adoptive mothers. Rather, most Russia-adoptive mothers strategically sought out connections that would either help facilitate Russian culture or allow for adoptive mothering support, but they were not seeking lifelong friends or fictive-kin relationships. For example, when telling me about her experiences with other Russia-adoptive families, Arlene Albright emphasized, "It's an effort. It's not necessarily great fun for me. A lot of these parents, it's not like they're *my* friends and I have a lot of things in common with them. But we do have one major thing in common: that our children were all adopted from the same or similar countries. And to me that's important because if I had been adopted I would want to have that connection and just have the information available and to know that there were other kids in the same situation."

Arlene's characterization of participation in the Russian adoption community as "effort" and "not great fun" was typical of many Russia-adoptive mothers and contrasts sharply with the way in which China-adoptive mothers spoke of the enjoyment and deep friendships they forged with other China adopters. Like China-adoptive mothers, those with Russian children looked to the groups as sources of friendship for their children, and they worked to maintain or facilitate connections with other adopted children. Arlene went on to say, "It's important for me because I want [my daughter] to be connected with other children when she gets older so that she feels that she's not alone—that there are a lot of other children that have this background, that were adopted from Russia."

The minority of Russia-adoptive mothers who were highly involved in culture keeping placed special importance on the connections their children had with other children who came from the same orphanage in Russia and whom their children had known prior to adoption. Theresa Fischer explained that she and her husband want their son "to be proud of being Russian and we feel like we want to honor the life he had over there and his birth parents." As a result, "It's very important to us that he have [and] maintain his friendship with a friend he knew before he knew Dennis and I."

As detailed in the previous chapter, motivation for Russian culture keeping centers on the absent birth mother. Orphanage mates, as de facto family, are seen an extension of the original birth family. By encouraging fictive kin friendships with orphanage mates, adoptive parents such as Theresa maintain their children's connections to Russia, to birth families, and to their origins. These types of fictive kin relationships, however, were much rarer among Russia-adoptive families than China-adoptive ones.

The Place of Culture

The difference in the level of adoptive family friendships experienced by women with children from Russia and those with children from China speaks to a larger general issue: the place birth culture holds in families' lives.

Among women with children from China, a China-adoptive cultural identity often largely overshadows the white ethnic affiliations of the parents. It was not uncommon for China-adoptive mothers to tell me "We are a Chinese American family." In this statement, the mothers were not expressing the sentiment that they had become Chinese American themselves. When asked, participants strongly denied having become Chinese American. Several women even physically recoiled when asked. Rather, in calling their families "Chinese American," they meant to express the dual identities of Chinese and American in their families, but in terms of both a unified family identity and a nomenclature more reflective of the actual ethnic practices in which these families engaged, it would have been more accurate for them to call themselves "China-Adoptive American" families.

Being a "China-Adoptive American" family translated into China-adoptive-related activities receiving preference over other activities formerly of importance to parents. Stacey Dita told me that, in her youth, doing temple and certain Jewish holidays "wasn't a huge part of our lives but it certainly is important to who I am," but "when I had to decide between Chinese dance and Hebrew school—and with a lot of guilt, believe me [*laughter*], because I have friends who are doing both—I felt like Chinese dance just felt like a better thing for her."

Some families with children from China (albeit none in my sample) have even relocated to China in order to better engage with Chinese culture. Others add Chinese elements to non-Chinese cultural or religious activities celebrated in the family. For example, at one adoption conference I attended, a China-adoptive mother spoke of hanging yin and yang symbols from the family *sukkah* (hut) during the Jewish holiday of Sukkot (harvest festival).

Among my sample there was a privileging of Chinese identity, activities, and elements over those associated with the ethnic heritage of the parents. "Chinese-ness," for example, is emphasized in family rituals. This can be seen in the important place Chinese holidays hold among China-adoptive families. All the China-adoptive families in the study celebrated Chinese New Year, and several also participated in the autumn moon festival. Many families held parties for these holidays or attended functions hosted either by FCC or other, smaller adoption groups.

Many families also brought China into their day-to-day lives through food. Most families ate Chinese food fairly regularly—venturing into Chinatown, picking up take-out from a local restaurant, or cooking it themselves at home. Several mothers had become proficient Chinese cooks. Not all the families enjoyed Chinese cuisine, but most found incorporating Chinese ingredients or dishes into their family meals to be an important part of authentically expressing their families' Chinese character within the rhythm of day-to-day family life.

Among China-adoptive families, the culture keeping strategies of food and holidays took them outside of their family circle, outside of their home, and drew them into interactions with others. For example, many women brought holiday lessons into their children's classes at school. Most of the mothers went into the schools and led activities with their children's classes related to a Chinese holiday (usually Chinese New Year). In order to do this, the mothers had to study about the holidays and learn the specifics on how to celebrate them. They relied upon FCC, other adoptive mothers, the internet, and books on Chinese celebrations in order to learn the various components of these holidays. Armed with this new information, they went into their children's classrooms and led exercises, made food, and read books in order to expose their children's classmates and teachers to Chinese culture.

These cultural lessons were intended to help facilitate the integration and acceptance of their children in their classrooms. By embarking on these lessons, China-adoptive mothers became the resident experts on China for their children's schools. Some even noted that Chinese American parents would seek their advice on the proper customs for Chinese holiday celebrations. For Russia-adoptive mothers engaged in culture keeping, taking on the child's "baggage," as Kerry Mead called it, also meant adapting and reshaping familial cultural traditions and practices. Unlike families with children from China, however, parents engaging with Russian culture did not let it supplant their own heritage. Rather, Russian practices were added to already existing ones. Following the basic tenet of multiculturalism, Russia-adoptive mothers engaged in culture keeping honored the cultural heritages of all the members of their families. For example, Theresa Fischer, a mother of Scandinavian ancestry, said that "if anything Russian crops up, we always look at it with interest and see if this something that Dimitri would enjoy or that we'd like to include in our family. Always with the intent of making sure he knows his traditions are as important as ours. And he shares in the Scandinavian ones too. It is sort of—but we are a family, so we do the Russian things, he does the Scandinavian things. And they are all a part of us."

The simultaneous practice of Russian and parental cultures was facilitated by what the mothers viewed as shared ethnic similarities. Of her family, Judy Inman, for example, spoke of the similarities in Czech and Russian cooking as a conduit to culture keeping: "It seemed to me that it was going to be much easier to incorporate Russian culture because there was so much Czech culture already in my family, even like in the cooking and everything. I've done a lot of Russian cooking, and it's very similar to Czech."

Like China-adoptive families, Russia-adoptive families have used food and holidays to engage in culture keeping. Theresa and Dennis Fischer have an annual Christmas party at which they incorporate the Russian tradition of the Babushka. Judy Inman's family has incorporated a "Name Day" holiday popular in Russia into their annual celebration of their daughter's adoption.

For the Russia-adoptive families in my sample, however, the strategies of incorporating food and holidays were largely based within the home. None of the mothers, for example, spoke of providing lessons on Russia or Russian culture for their children's classrooms, whereas nearly all of the China-adoptive mothers did.

The ways that China- and Russia-adoptive mothers engage their families in these two popular modes of cultural enactment—food and holidays—point to important differences in these communities. For China-adoptive mothers, food and holidays were largely group-oriented events that connected them to the Chinese adoption community. For Russia-adoptive families, the consumption of Russian food and the celebration of Russian holidays were not mechanisms through which they connected with other families with children from Russia or with members of the Russian community. "Culture" for the China-adoptive families can be seen, therefore, to be largely public (and visible), while for Russia-adoptive families it is largely familial (and hidden).

Racial Considerations

In some obvious and some more nuanced ways, race directly shaped these basic differences in the mothers' thinking about and participation in culture keeping. The interracial aspect of families with children from China and the monoracial aspect of families with children from Russia propelled the China group toward culture keeping and the Russia group away from it.

For the China group, understandings of race underpinned culture keeping in two distinct ways. First, culture keeping was an active strategy mothers employed to *protect* their children from the effects of race, namely racial identity issues they fear will arise in adolescence. These women learned the importance of keeping culture for their racial minority children in the context of adoption. The historical debates surrounding domestic transracial adoption and the more recent response regarding race, culture, and family by Korean adoptees have shaped how the international adoption community as a whole and individual adoptive parents think about birth culture. Unlike women of color parenting biological children, however, these mothers were most concerned about *future* problems regarding race. These women anticipated that self-esteem garnered through culture identity work would help protect their children from feelings of alienation due to their racial and ethnic minority status during their teenage years.

Although many mothers did become the resident Chinese "experts" for their children's classrooms, the racial safety duties for the majority of these women did not include moving their families to more racially diverse neighborhoods or schools, nor did it involve concerted efforts to engage in systematic and personal ways with the Chinese community. While some families did live in neighborhoods with some racial diversity (generally white and Asian), these parents raised their children in relative *social* segregation despite *residential* integration. Few of the families had Asian friends and, as described earlier, although they desired intimate relationships with Chinese ethnics, most experienced a deep awkwardness in their attempts to connect.

Second, culture keeping among the China group was a way to *give* their children racialized identities. These mothers saw the process of international adoption stripping their daughters of intimate cultural knowledge and ties to a rich ethnic heritage. Culture keeping was a way to reconnect their children to this interrupted racial and ethnic identity. This objective was shaped by the Asian "ethnic expectation" (Tuan 1998) described earlier—that, because the children look Chinese, they should possess the ability to act Chinese (even if they choose not to do so). Chinese-looking children are asked by strangers to display their Chinese-ness (for example, people ask, "Do you use chopsticks? Do you like rice? Do you speak Chinese?" or talk to them in Chinese and question their knowledge of Chinese history and geography), and these women wanted their children to be prepared to meet this expectation. The mothers wanted their children to possess an adequate degree of Chinese cultural competency despite the fact that they were being raised by white parents in overwhelmingly white worlds. The main mode of cultural transmission they preferred was participation in the China adoption community.

Race also shapes the culture keeping of women with children from Russia. The minority of Russia-adoptive mothers engaged in culture keeping worked to establish a Russian ethnic identity in their children. They value birth culture and feel that it is necessary in order to facilitate a healthy self-esteem in children who experienced abandonment and (birth) mother loss. They conceive of their mothering responsibilities to entail Russian culture, and they work to ensure it is entwined in the lives and identities of their children.

Unlike the China group however, their culture keeping is not motivated by racism or racial identity politics. Rather it centers on a deep appreciation and interest in culture per se. Following the basic tenet of multiculturalism, these women honored the cultural heritages of all members in their families. The parents in these families asserted their own ethnic identities alongside those of their adopted children and they engaged in the related multiple culture practices. In essence they enjoyed ethnicity—the food, the holidays, the feeling of ethnic affinity—and wanted their children to do so as well. As Kerry Mead shared, "Just like I'm proud of my Irish ancestry, I think she should be proud of her Russian ancestry."

In this way, the culture keeping of Russia-adoptive mothers closely resembles the symbolic ethnicity of later generation white ethnics. However, culture keeping for these women was not purely recreational, as it was also shaped by their concerns about the effects institutionalization and abandonment by birth mothers had on their children. Connecting their children to Russian culture was seen as a way to help children cope with both that initial parental rejection by their birth mother, the separation from their birth families, and the consequential institutionalization. Unlike symbolic ethnicity, culture keeping among Russia-adoptive mothers was explicitly about instilling a positive self-esteem in their children.

The majority of women in the Russia group, however, did not attempt to teach their children much beyond rudimentary information about Russia. These children were not expected to participate in Russian cultural activities or to be able to display cultural competency. There were women who held ideological commitments to multiculturalism and culture keeping but who had a difficult time putting those beliefs into practice. Others more openly downplayed the importance of culture keeping (while at the same time giving it lip service).

The majority of women with children from Russia minimized ethnic differences between themselves and their children in order to facilitate familial connectedness. They did this through emphasizing cultural similarity in the ethnic heritages of themselves, their husbands, and their children. Most importantly, they encouraged a white American racial identity, which they shared with their children, to eclipse what they reported to be divisive ethnic and national identities.

Conclusion

This chapter has examined the ways in which decisions about culture keeping are shaped by concerns over difference. International-adoptive mothers seek to normalize difference for their children through the decisions they make about culture. For China-adoptive mothers, the difference between "Chinese-ness" and "American-ness" is racialized. This racial difference is not only of their children from themselves but of themselves from Chinese. The strategy mothers use to address this racial difference is ethnic—they attend to race through engaging in and developing a China-adoptive ethnicity. And they seek to normalize participation in Chinese ethnicity, and to make that experience as "authentic" as possible, through primarily engaging in it in the company of other white adoptive families.

For Russia-adoptive mothers the difference between "Russian-ness" and "American-ness" is seen as ethnic, not racial. The strategy that the majority of Russia-adoptive mothers use to deal with this ethnic difference is racial—they seek to integrate their children into their families and communities through emphasizing racial similarity. Moreover, those who do practice Russia-adoptive culture familialize it. Russia-adoptive culture is not institutionalized in the same way that we can find China-adoptive culture. Rather, it is largely practiced within the home. Connections between white ethnic familial identities are emphasized. Any ethnic difference that could be made strongly visible through engagement in culture keeping in a more public setting is avoided.

Aspects of what is usually understood to comprise culture are clearly absent from China- and Russia-adoptive culture. Adoptive culture is not about particular values, beliefs, morals, or family structure. Rather, adoptive mothers focus on more tangible aspects of culture, such as food, holidays, toys, knick-knacks, and books. This is a popular route to ethnic cultural engagement among many in the United States.

For China-adoptive families, because of their own ethnic distance from China prior to adoption, that culture is largely accessed and practiced in semi-public spheres that have been familialized (the fictive family of the China adoption community). Because this version of culture requires public display, it lends itself easily to commercialization and consumerism and has become big business. The 2007 catalog for China Sprout, one of the largest purveyors of China goods for the adoption community, for example, boasts eighty-six pages of various Chinese-related goods, ranging from talking Chinese dictionaries to leather wallets embossed with Chairman Mao's calligraphy. Especially popular are items with the Chinese calligraphy for "mother" and "daughter." This "Chinese culture" is neatly packaged and sold to international-adoptive parents.

Because of the public nature of Chinese culture keeping, China-adoptive mothers are easily able to "plug into" the China-adoptive community and ascribed notions of culture. Some women indicated to me that they were merely following protocol and had not individually critiqued or constructed the route through which they kept culture. They merely did "what everyone else does." They were grateful for other mothers who decided on the travel group reunions and FCC local playdates because they "simply had to show up." Contemporary China-adoptive mothers are told by their agencies that they should keep culture and then, through the China-adoptive community that has developed since the mid-1990s, they are presented with an easily accessible, friendly, and enjoyable route to do so.

This is the focus of much culture keeping: community and belonging. For China-adoptive mothers, that community is a China-adoptive one. China-adoptive mothers cannot hide difference because it is racialized in their families and so seek to normalize it by primarily engaging with other families who mirror their own. The majority of Russia-adoptive mothers can hide difference (if they so desire—and many do because they see it as in the best interest of their children) because it is ethnic, not racial. The majority familialize any culture keeping within their intimate family spheres. It is integration into the familial and neighborhood context that shapes (dis)engagement with Russian culture. Although many Russia-adoptive mothers reported envy for the organized events and community connections available to the China-adoptive community, few felt emboldened to facilitate changes in their mode of culture keeping (making it more public, for example) that would cast light upon the differences in ethnic origins within their families.

In these variations between China and Russia culture keeping, we can see how in culture keeping mothers deliberately work at the negotiation of difference by facilitating a positive and tangible ethnic identity for their children—an identity that is based on inclusion in a family (Russia) or community (China) of others who share that identity.

5

Adoptive Families in the Public Eye

Parents of children with a different ethnicity constantly
get asked questions by curious people, some friendly, some
ignorant, some that are eager to share their own history.
However, the implicit message, no matter how well intended the
question, always is "you don't look like you belong together."
Please think about that next time you have the urge to ask.

The plea above was shared by "Anne," a reader commenting on the *New York Times* adoption blog series, *Relative Choices* (*relativechoices.blogs.nytimes.com*). In this series, eleven adoptive parents, birth mothers, and adoptees shared thought-provoking essays on adoption. The comment above was in response to Jeff Gammage's contribution, "A Normal Family" (December 2, 2007). Gammage, a white China-adoptive father and reporter for *The Philadelphia Inquirer,* wrote of the questions he receives in public from both strangers to adoption and those involved in the adoption world who are curious about the relationship he has with his Chinese-born daughters. By December 6, four days after his essay was originally published, Gammage's post had generated 118 responses. Some commenters, like the one above, wrote in to support Gammage; some thanked him for articulating their experiences so well. Others just as forcefully commented that people who pose questions to adoptive families are merely curious and well-meaning. These commenters argued that everyone gets asked questions when out and about with their children and that Gammage should just "lighten up."

The heart of Gammage's essay and the battle of wills in its comments section point to how family form shapes the tenor of public interactions. When in public, all families are on display, open to unsolicited comment from strangers—to questions, stares, even violence—or conversely the lack of such attention due to their family form or the behavior of individual family members. This monitoring is especially acute when adults are in public with young children. In this surveillance of family form and behavior, we see how parents are held accountable for their ability to comply with familial norms.

Norms about the family are, of course, variable; they are not static nor are they identical across communities. The idea that the white, middle-class, monoracial, heterosexual family constitutes the only *real* "American Family" is shifting—somewhat. There are places in the country, for example, where interracial, adopted, blended, single or gay parent families are, if not the norm, then widely seen, tolerated, and even accepted. In other communities, however, these "nonnormative" families are actively discouraged, sometimes through violence. This chapter examines how the white, middle-class mothers in New England who spoke with me—members of families who do not match the hegemonic "American Family" along the lines of monoraciality and biological kinship—have public encounters that speak to ideological norms of the family.

The Interracial Surveillance of China-Adoptive Families

The families with children adopted from China who spoke with me drew considerable attention in public spaces—attention that suggests that others are engaged in the surveillance of families to assess the degree to which they fit the ideological normative family mold. White adoptive parents in my study reported a surveillance they felt when out in public with their Asian children. This surveillance was characterized by a near constant trickle of inquiries directed at them in public spaces—grocery stores, playgrounds, airplanes, parking lots—about their adoption experiences and their children. The questions families receive range from the innocuous to the offensive. Lorraine Burg described this attention and the burden she felt it placed on her family:

> So everywhere we go people look twice at us and it has become sort of the norm. So we're used to it. But people ask questions, you know: "Is she your daughter?" "Is your husband Chinese?" They ask her, you know, other kids say, "That's not your real mother." So all of those things sort of impact us more than any other piece, just because it's so daily and so constant.

It is the interracial aspect of these families and what it signals to others—nonbiological kinship and international adoption—that drives this surveillance. Unlike families (either biological or adopted) in which all members appear to be biologically related due to shared racial classifications, the members of these families feel as if they cannot hide their nonbiological mode of family formation. Others most often read the racial makeup of these families (white parents, Asian children) to represent transracial adoption, rather than an alternative route to whites parenting Asian children: Asian/white intimate partnering. The obviousness of their route to family formation stems in part from cultural understandings of biological race and the near invisibility of interracial Asian/white families in mainstream American public consciousness. These Chinese children are "obviously" adopted because cultural understandings of race and the family do not include the possibility of a white woman giving birth to an Asian child.[1]

This is particularly poignant when one parent is out alone with his or her child(ren) and, therefore, the racial status of the other assumed parent unknown to strangers. As Rachel Abramson explained, the fact of adoption cannot be concealed for these families—even as they humorously skirt the possibility of being taken for a member of an Asian/white romantic couple: "I cannot pretend that she's not adopted. Although sometimes I think when I'm just alone they might think my husband's Chinese. [*laughter*] But it is always out there. We are always [being asked], 'Is she your real daughter?' We are always getting these obnoxious questions."

The questions families receive focus on clarifying or fixing the nature of the relationship between adult and child: *Are they really related? Why are they together? Why is this white woman mothering this Asian child in public?* I call these types of encounters "interracial surveillance"—a phenomenon by which interracial families or multiracial individuals draw public interest and are scrutinized, monitored, or harassed because they embody multiple racial positions.[2] Interracial surveillance is similar to "border patrolling" that Heather Dalmage notes is "a form of discrimination faced by those who cross the color line, do not stick with their own, or attempt to claim membership (or are placed by others) in more than one racial group" (Dalmage 2007, 218). However, while border patrolling takes many forms and occurs in multiple settings, including private interactions between family members (Dalmage 2000), interracial surveillance, as defined here, focuses specifically on the monitoring of families and individuals by *strangers* in *public settings.*

The interracial surveillance of international adoptive families has a unique tenor. It is unlike the surveillance of U.S. black/white intimate relations, both in what it includes and in what it excludes. Although black/white couples report public interest and fascination about their relationships, they also detail being ignored or receiving an edgy hostility directed at them resulting in poor service, cold stares, epithets, and violence in public spaces (Azoulay 1997; Childs 2005; Dalmage 2000 and 2007; Reddy 1996). Indeed, a desire to circumvent this type of interracial surveillance plays a role in the selection of China for adoption. As noted earlier, the popularity of international adoption is partially fueled by a desire to avoid the domestic adoption of black children. There were a variety of reasons participants in my study desired not to adopt across the black/white divide, including familial prejudice and a sensitivity to the contentious debate surrounding the efficacy of whites raising blacks in a racist society. Participants in my study also indicated a strong desire to circumvent what they imagined to be an intensely negative interracial surveillance that they felt would result from the adoption of black children.

Pre-adoption, parents felt comfortable with the level of interracial surveillance they imagined their new white/Asian families would experience. What they experienced post-adoption, however, was an almost constant interest in them, with strangers wanting to learn the intimate details of their families' lives. While some of the women came to terms with this intrusive surveillance, none reported it a thorough pleasure, and many experienced it as an assault of a sort. Although the families in my study weren't literally physically "accosted" (which has been an issue in other cases of interracial surveillance), many used that language to describe their public encounters, even if recalling them with humor. More so than any one interaction in particular, it was the bluntness and the consistency—in both form and occurrence—of these encounters that characterized them as intrusive. While the families in my study rarely if ever experienced a directly hateful or racist remark, they were made aware of their nonnormative families in the blunt repetitive questions they received: *Where is she from? Are you her mother? How much did she cost? Is she adopted? She's so cute; does she speak Chinese?* While study participants indicated they circulated in largely white, middle-class worlds, they did receive these seemingly innocuous questions from people from varying social locations in all manner of public settings—often multiple times in one outing.

The interracial surveillance experienced by international-adoptive families with Asian children can be thought of, in essence, as one of attraction, while that of biological black/white families can largely be seen as one of repulsion.[3] Both, however, serve to Other (de Beauvoir 1984; Kristeva 1991) interracial families by communicating the idea of familial difference and norm violation. Parallels can be made to Foucault's "normalizing gaze," characterized by "a surveillance that makes it possible to qualify, to classify and to punish" by "observing hierarchy" and "normalizing judgment" (1977, 184). Interracial families are publicly gazed upon through a normative family lens and held accountable for their apparent differences by unsolicited attention being drawn to their nonnormative familial form—inscribed on their bodies through "race." They are made to account for their differences by consistently being asked to explain them to others as they go about their daily lives.

Adoptive parents with children from China use a variety of strategies to deal with interracial surveillance. Crafty mothers shut down conversations ("I'm sorry we have to go"), deflect questions, "dodge" possible conversations by moving away from people at the grocery store (or state fair, doctor's office, park, etcetera), or avert their eyes from interested strangers. At times, mothers refuse to answer questions coming at them from strangers. Nancy Thorne laughed as she told of how she tried to avoid answering questions from several women hounding her:

I remember this one woman chasing us in a grocery store when we were in Capital City. [I said] "I'm not going to talk about this! Leave me alone!" The second person just wanted to know like everything. "Have you ever heard of boundaries? Why am I going to tell you all of this? I'm just now figuring out how to go grocery shopping with a baby! Okay? I haven't figured this all out yet!" [*laughter*]

An important and telling strategy was refusing to "understand" the nature of the question. This was used most often when presented with a direct question, such as "Is she your daughter?" or "Are you her real mother?" The participants in my study understood the nature of the question: the strangers were asking about biological kinship. In these inquiries about authentic relationships, the China-adoptive mothers understood the real questions: "Is she your *biological* daughter?" and "Are you her *biological* mother?"

A strategy the mothers used was to refuse to acknowledge the intent of the question and rather to respond in the affirmative: "Yes, she is my daughter." "Yes, I am her real mother." "Yes, they really are sisters." By doing this, the mothers defined adoptive relationships as *real* kinship. Shannon Lynch shared such a story. In addition to being a China-adoptive parent, she is the aunt of an adopted Chinese girl. When her niece was three or four, they were together in a car with the windows open. Seeing them, a man in a convertible yelled, "Is she adopted?" Lynch looked at him, said "She's my niece," and closed up the window.

This strategy of offended or witty reply was especially useful when receiving the "blue ribbon" of supermarket surveillance questions: "How much did she cost?" Adoptive parents particularly dislike and/or fear this question as it touches a nerve—that of the commodification of children and of baby-buying (Dorow 2006a). Participants would respond "not nearly enough" or "priceless" or "about the same as a C-section." This refusal to "understand" the nature of the question is an act of resistance (Stiers 2007) through which parents reject the definition of non-biological kinship as second-best.

Interracial surveillance often took the form of paying compliments to children about their appearance such as, "What a cutie! Does she speak Chinese?" Although the mothers in my study did not deny that their daughters were good-looking, and many even gushed unapologetically about their children, they found this continual "positive" attention from strangers problematic, as they believed it relied on Asian fetishization. The mothers were worried that so much fawning would direct their children to a particular type of self-identification (such as "cute little Asian kid"). They didn't want their daughters to understand their value or worthiness only in their ability to be attractive. Holly Pritchard, worried about her daughter privileging looks over intelligence, countered such comments with ones that praised her academic ability, such as "well yes, she's really good in school, too."

The mothers also reported that this attention from strangers focused on appearance made the connection for their children between their bodily features—which physicalize their "Chinese-ness" and which can not altered (at least not without the aid of cosmetic surgery)—and difference. Leanne Becker noted the consequence of this kind of attention was "a lot like somebody coming up to you and saying, 'You stick out like a sore thumb, and I think it's great.'" They didn't want their daughters made to feel always like "a sore thumb," even if that difference was defined positively. Lynn Werden discussed her approach to the flattering compliments paid to her daughter:

> Because in a certain way you don't want all that curiosity
> and attention focused on your family as if you're some

amazing beauty or something. So, you know, I guess [I respond with] some combination of answering, some combination of avoiding, but really trying just to be really matter-of-fact and really happy in that, "Yes, she's a beautiful child," blah, blah but just trying to normalize it and kind of keep it cloaked in.

Despite the fact that China-adoptive mothers were often irritated with the interracial surveillance they experienced, they did note several positive features associated with being a visibly adoptive family. They saw public interactions as opportunities for educating prospective adopters about adoption from China. As Eloise Nolan noted, "People ask, and they don't always ask just to be nosy." Parents understood that people touched by adoption—especially those in the midst of the adoption process—desire to connect with someone who has been through the experience. Because study participants were aware of this, they reported replying to inquiries with, "Why do you ask?" or "Do you know someone who has adopted?"

China-adoptive mothers also temper strong or negative reactions to interracial surveillance out of concern for the reputation of international adoption and interracial families. As Holly Pritchard explained, she wanted to act as a positive spokesperson for adoptive families:

People are just nosy, but I don't think—I don't believe people are doing it maliciously, and certainly not consciously. They aren't consciously being intrusive. They just don't see that they are being intrusive. And I don't think it helps international adoption, in general, and mixed—multiracial families, in general, to blow them off, because then they're just—then they go home with an attitude of, you know, in the back of their minds it was a negative experience . . . But generally speaking I try to handle them in a positive way, because I just think you can cause more damage refusing it. I really don't—I sincerely don't think people are doing it intentionally to put you on the spot.

Through interracial surveillance, China-adoptive parents thus learn to act as educators and find themselves in the position of promoting international adoption. Many women found themselves willing, though not necessarily pleased, to take on this role.

Another form of education was also practiced when basic social norms regarding privacy of families—especially those granted to middle-class whites—are transgressed by interracial surveillance (see Fox 1999 on social norms of privacy). Women resist interracial surveillance by reminding the offending party of these social norms. That education can be more overt, but often falls on deaf ears. When family members do attempt to extend lessons on privacy, they often attempt a balance of power in the information exchange: they demand the same information of the asking party. But as Leanne Becker's story illustrates, the questions—and the entitled right people feel to ask them and receive answers—are unidirectional in that those asking the questions do not expect to be questioned in turn:

You know, [strangers] are very well-meaning, but they don't expect those same questions to be asked of them. In fact my daughter, my older daughter, once did. Somebody came up to us and said, "Where is she from?" and I said, "Well, she was born in China." [My daughter] said, "And where are you from?" and the woman started laughing like this was a ridiculous question, because of course, to her, it was. [It was as if this woman was saying], "Why would you ask? I'm white." [*laughter*] "I belong here. You don't."

As many mothers noted, most people who ask these questions of adoptive families in public are unaware of how they are received. Therefore, as Leanne's story illustrates, direct resistance to interracial surveillance is often itself misunderstood, and either ignored or met with baffled silence.

An interesting dynamic of the interracial surveillance experienced by international-adoptive families is that it changes over time for individual families. The parents of older children deal less frequently with direct, intrusive questions from other adults such as "How much did she cost?" This can be attributed to social norms about interactions concerning children: questions about babies and toddlers are addressed to their adult companions, but questions about older children are often directed to the children themselves.

The families in my study had all adopted in the 1990s; many characterized themselves as on "the cutting edge" of international adoption. One could speculate that, with more international-adoptive families in the public eye, people have become less likely to regard international adoption as unique and worthy of comment. However, my time in the field with recent adoptive families contradicts this idea. On websites, at conferences, and in public venues such as the *New York Times* adoption blog, the topic of how to handle intrusive questions continues to be popular. Interracial surveillance remains as much an issue for newly formed families as it was for those who adopted a decade ago. Therefore, I see the ages of the children affecting the comments their parents receive—more so than the increased popularity of adoption.

Although, as their children grew older, the participants in my study fielded fewer comments associated with interracial surveillance from adult strangers, they spoke of an increase in questions, stares, and comments from other children. For example, Charlotte Gordon recounted how, at a playground in her multiracial neighborhood, a black child asked her and her daughter, "What are you doing together?" Despite the decrease in comments from adults, the mothers of older children felt they had to become even more vigilant than before about their responses to public encounters—especially to questions with racist or anti-adoption overtones—since their children were able to comprehend the questions being asked and to evaluate the ways in which their parents reacted. The mothers framed their replies specifically with their children in mind, regardless of how complete or appropriate a questioning party might or might not find their answers; since their children would hear what they said and how they said it, they wanted to respond "proudly and calmly," as Nancy Thorne put it.

An important positive feature of the visibility of adoptive families with children from China is that it allows adoptive families to find each other, to connect, and to seek support through recognition of each other in public spaces. As Mitchell Sorokin told me, "When you adopt a Chinese baby it's pretty obvious. It's not like you're adopting from some other countries [where] you can almost kind of get away with [pretending as if] they're your biological kids. People know you're an adoptive parent and you can spot each other in the malls and stuff. You kind of give each other the little wink or something—that kind of thing."

Parents like Mitchell enjoy their families' being recognized as adoptive families by other adoptive parents; such encounters have sometimes led to deep and abiding friendships. Thus, ironically, adoptive parents themselves may engage in the same type of behavior they bemoan in others. They may utter complaints similar to Charlotte Gordon's "Sometimes I just can't stand another goddamned idiot comment," while at the same time approaching each other when out and about to ask, "Where is she from?" The complicated terrain of adoptive visibility means that, although being "put on the spot" (as Holly

Pritchard characterized it) is indeed what does occur through interracial surveillance, that spot often serves as an important site for educating others about adoption, locating friends, and network-building among other adoptive families with children from China.

The Quasi-Biological Privilege of Russia-Adoptive Families

In stark contrast to the experiences of China-adoptive families, unless Russia-adoptive families consciously mark themselves, they are, in essence, invisible to strangers as adoptive families or as families with a child born in Russia. Because of shared race, participants in the study with children from Russia remarked that they were often mistaken in public as being biological parents to their adopted children. This was most often displayed through comments regarding physical resemblance between parent and child. Dotty Cohen described how her daughters, adopted from Russia, are viewed when they are out in public: "My daughters walk around and no one looks at them. I mean, they look a little like me—I don't think it's paramount—or a lot like me but they resemble us enough that people on the street would never say, 'Oh, okay' " (i.e., "That's an adoptive family").

This imagined biological link is attractive. Esther Levenson confided that she found it very exciting when people said she and her son looked "sort of similar." Part of the excitement for adoptive parents is experiencing normative parenting: for many biological parents, discussions about physical resemblance between parent and child play a prominent role in public interactions.

In a society that privileges biological relatedness between parent and child—especially between mother and child—and problematizes other types of parent/child kinship (adoptive/ foster/stepparenting), the ability to appear as if one is biologically related to one's child confers special benefits. I call this "biological privilege." This term is popularly used to describe the ability of women to conceive and bear children. I play on that usage when I employ the term to conceptualize not the fact of biologically birthing a child but the privilege of appearing *as if* one has done so. Regardless of visible mothering behavior, biological privilege is *not* granted to all mothers who have birthed their children, but only to those who appear phenotypically similar enough to their children to be classified readily as a biological mother. White biological mothers of children of color, for example, are denied this privilege whenever their relationships to their children are questioned. This demonstrates the way in which biological privilege is explicitly rooted in normative understandings of the family as a racialized unit—of who is and who can be biologically related to others. Interracial surveillance and biological privilege, therefore, are flip sides of the same coin.

Biological privilege is granted to both individuals and to families, and translates most directly into a notion of familial privacy—of anonymity in public spaces because one adheres to the norm of biological relatedness in families. Individuals and families who hold biological privilege are granted public support for the form their familial relationships take. This can be seen in the public experiences of parents with children adopted from Russia. As a consequence of their ability to appear biologically related to their children, the status of parents with children from Russia is not publicly questioned by strangers. White Russia-adoptive parents are able to move freely in public with their white Russian-born children without questions or stares by strangers. They do not receive questions regarding how they came to be a family, nor do the children receive special attention. The shared racial status of the family members allow the privilege of anonymity. The families in my study who adopted from Russia experienced what I call "quasi-biological privilege," in that their adoptive status was invisible to strangers.

In theory, because it's widely assumed that phenotypically similar parents and children are biogenetically related, parents who adopt monoracially have available to them the choice either to divulge or keep hidden their adoptive status. Today's adoption practices, however, do not allow for the secrecy and sealed records that were so prominent in the earlier twentieth century (Carp 1998; Pertman 2000; Melosh 2002). Full disclosure of adoption, especially to the adopted child, is now strongly promoted. This is current standard practice in adoption, and anything less is regarded as cause for concern among adoption workers (Melosh 2002). Bonnie Hill believed that an orientation toward concealment would be enough to disqualify one for adoption: "I think that, if you said to an adoption agency that you were not going to talk about it, you would not get approved."

Cautionary tales of the difficulties experienced by adult adoptees discovering their origins late in life also frame and propel prescribed disclosure. The parents in my study argued that it would be considered taboo to hide the fact of adoption from their children, as doing so would be psychologically damaging to them. Given these contemporary notions about how best to treat the issue of adoption, it is not surprising that all the parents in my sample—both China- and Russia-adoptive mothers—were open with their children about the fact that they were adopted. At an early age, these children were informed about how they came to be members of their families. Mothers were emphatic that adoption be discussed with and processed by their children. Even among Russia-adoptive families, parents actively pulled back the biological scrim *within their homes* in order to fulfill their responsibilities to openness and honesty.

In *public encounters,* however, adoption disclosure for families with children from Russia varied. Unlike the families with children from China, whose adoptive status was seemingly "obvious" to all, those with children from Russia could choose to divulge or hide their adopted status to strangers. Because of shared phenotype, however, these families actually had fewer occasions for naturally bringing up adoption in public encounters. Opportunities for disclosure did arise, however, when comments about physical resemblance were made. Kerry Mead spoke of people saying things like, "Oh, she looks just like you." Depending on the commenter, she and her daughter would either tell them about the adoption or simply respond with an amused "Oh, thank you."

The parents in my study with children from Russia were emphatic that adoption was not something that should be hidden out of embarrassment. They often expressed delight when their children openly and enthusiastically shared their adoption stories with strangers, such as when Dennis Fischer went bowling with his son: "A girl next to us in the next alley had seen that his name was Dimitri and said what a great name that was and immediately Dimitri said, 'Well, I'm from Russia. I was adopted at two from an orphanage.'" The parents were also familiar, however, with the intrusive questions or inappropriate comments that sometimes follow exposure as an adoptive family. Carol Acher articulated the dilemma between disclosure and protection: "We're very open about [adoption], but some people can say things that aren't very smart to say in front of a four-year-old." The choice the parents with children from Russia faced in public encounters therefore was not only between celebrating adoption or privileging biology, but between protecting familial privacy or exposing themselves to the possibility of intrusive questions or inappropriate comments. In the sometimes-taken choice to maintain the scrim of biology, we can see the privilege of privacy granted to families who match the hegemonic family norm of monoraciality signaling (seemingly) biological kinship.

Quasi-biological privilege protected Russia-adoptive families from interracial surveillance, but this lack of adoptive visibility was not always completely welcomed. Parents reported that it kept others from "truly seeing" their families as adoptive, which translated into a source of isolation. Many Russia-adoptive parents spoke with envy about the community available to China-adoptive families through spontaneous encounters in public settings. (Recall the wink in the mall that Mitchell Sorokin mentioned.) Bonnie Hill articulated this dilemma:

> I would go to playgrounds and I would see these *very adopted families*. I mean it was like, "Oh, okay." And . . . I'd go with my son and there would be no identifying mark. But if I had shown up with a South American child, or an Asian child, you know, it would be like having "A for Adopted" stamped someplace on your person, whereas that didn't happen . . . And I never knew what to do. I never knew whether to just go up to this other parent and say, "So, your kid is adopted. So is mine," you know, because it felt like that would be invading their privacy.

Although they enjoyed their freedom from interracial surveillance, the parents with children adopted from Russia did not have access to a visible adoptive status that would allow for them to approach people in what they felt to be a natural way. (Note Bonnie's "I never knew what to do" when she wanted to connect with a stranger over adoption.) In this way, quasi-biological privilege and the lack of interracial surveillance impeded them from feeling support from other adoptive families in public settings, feeling connected to the adoption community, and building friendship networks.

Conclusion

The experiences of international adoptive families in public spaces focus attention on important ways in which families are evaluated by others. Comparing the experiences of families with children from China and those with children from Russia illustrates the significance of race in family surveillance. Those families that are easily identified as international adoptive due to racial differences are objectified as interesting curiosities. This objectification does not result in structural discrimination or physical intimidation, but rather in a type of stigma that denies families privacy. The loss of privilege experienced by these families is symbolic of their status as different. As Goffman's work on stigma (1963) emphasized, the symbolic loss of normativity is not inconsequential. It is deeply experienced and can have material as well as social and psychological impacts.

Comparing the adoption decision-making of parents with children from China and Russia makes visible the nuanced and complicated relationships adopters have to both interracial surveillance and biological privilege. For many, part of the race equation was how the potential racial makeup of their families would influence the tenor of their day-to-day lives in public settings. This speaks to a larger issue in family formation. It shows how our choices of family members—who we choose to adopt, or even, perhaps, to form a committed relationship or to parent with—are influenced by anticipated surveillance and by expectations of how strangers in fleeting public encounters will react to our choices. The consistency of surveillance and the degree to which people seek information from adoptive families signal not only an interest but a cultural anxiety related to ambiguous and nonnormative family forms. Yet the experiences of interracial surveillance and biological privilege post-adoption are complex. For families with children from China, interracial surveillance is intrusive and annoying, but it also makes possible links between adoptive families. Likewise, quasi-biological privilege grants families with children from Russia anonymity; at the same time, they lack an acceptable public means to create new connections with other adoptive families.

The experiences of adoptive families in public make visible a constant surveillance of the family—all families—that holds us accountable to idealized norms. These norms, of course, vary by time and place. For example, in communities or contexts where interracial or adoptive families are the norm, we could imagine very different types of assessments. The participants in my study reported that it was precisely the supportive interactions regarding family form that drew them, for example, to adoptive family organizations. In public interactions, however, the continued dominance of monoraciality and biological kinship in normative ideas about the family heavily shaped the type of interactions they had with strangers. In their experiences, we can see the hegemonic "American Family" continuing to shape family life—especially among the white middle class—despite its anachronistic status.

6

Conclusion

Keeping Culture, Keeping Kin

Formal adoption in the United States presents an interesting mechanism that makes visible contentious issues regarding family formation and social stratification. The process of
moving children from one familial context to another taps into
ideologies and assessments of "parenting fitness," the "rights"
of children, and which kinds of children should be included or
excluded from belonging with which kinds of parents. These
issues, which are emotionally intense and sometimes volatile,
have a long history. In 1904, for example, forty white Irish
American children from a New York City Catholic orphanage
were transported via "orphan trains" to Arizona and placed
with Mexican Catholics. After only one night with their new
families, the children were forcibly removed by Anglo vigi-
lantes who felt duty-bound to "rescue" and redistribute them
among their Anglo neighbors. The children had been originally
placed with the Mexican families due to their shared Catholic
religion, but they were ultimately removed because they did
not racially or ethnically match—a move that was upheld by
the United States Supreme Court (Gordon 1999).

The "Great Arizona Orphan Abduction" (as it is called by
Linda Gordon in her book of the same name) is a dramatic
example of the ways in which battles over children in adop-

tion often occur in the context of race. This case was particularly remarkable as it not only involved interracial adoptions in the early twentieth century, but had white children originally placed with nonwhite parents. In contrast, racial "matching" has long been the historic norm in formal adoption (Melosh 2002), reflecting racial boundary crossing as a contentious issue in family formation.

Issues of race and belonging continue to shape contemporary family formation at the beginning of the twenty-first century. Debate persists, for example, over the proper permanent placement and care for racial and ethnic minority children in state care. Culture keeping developed as a response to the issues that swirl around the family as a racialized unit. It is largely an attempt to negotiate race and ethnicity and to normalize international adoptive families within a white, middle-class social milieu that characterizes them as different.

The family normalization process begins early. While all family formation in the United States occurs in the context of a socially stratified society, adoptive motherhood involves a conscious and intentional construction and maintenance of a family along the lines of race and ethnicity. Non-adoptive family formation also involves decisions along racial and ethnic lines. However, in adoption, parents must actually articulate what "type" of child (i.e., along the lines of race/ethnicity, gender, and disability) they would be willing to parent. This deliberate process forces women to consciously confront and articulate their perspectives on race, ethnicity, and family. For international adoptive families, because their adoptions transgress norms of biological kinship and racial matching that dominate white, middle-class discourse on families, they are often seen to symbolize progressive change on both micro and macro levels. Much of the literature on international adoption poses these placements as allowing for new ideas of race, ethnicity, and kinship to circulate within individual families, especially among white parents (Bates 1993; Evans 2000; Klose 1999; Newman 2001; Reddy 1996; Register 1991; Wolff 2000). Interracial families, in particular, are seen to potentially symbolize progressive new attitudes in the United States at a societal level regarding race (Bartholet 1999; Evans 2000; Lazarre 1996; Luke and Luke 1998; McBride 1996; McCabe 2003). Interracial marriage has longed been looked to as a barometer of race relations (Fryer 2007; Moran 2001); international adoption is now similarly characterized in the literature. What light does my research shed on these supposed shifts in the "American Family"? Does parenting an adopted child change one's feelings about race? Does it shift how one conceptualizes kinship? In examining these questions, I would like to return again to one of the most significant differences between the two groups of mothers: China culture keeping is public and visible, while Russia culture keeping is private and familial. With this in mind, the ways in which these two groups of women approached an act often expressive of ethnicity, the naming of their children, are striking.

Naming and Race

> The naming activity is ultimately a social process, and the resulting pattern of name usage reflects the combined influence of the imagery associated with each name, the notions parents have about the future characteristics of their children, estimates of the response others have to the name, the awareness and knowledge of names through mass media and other sources, parents' beliefs about what are appropriate children's names for persons of their status, and institutionalized norms and pressures.
> —Stanley Lieberson and Eleanor Bell (1992, 514)

The first names given to the adopted children of the women in this study are counterintuitive given the culture keeping activities enacted within the families. While the majority of mothers with children from Russia tended to downplay overt public displays of Russian culture, the naming of their children was one way in which the children's ethnic heritage was emphasized. Thirty-one percent of the Russia-adoptive mothers kept the birth (or orphanage) name of their children, and an additional 21 percent made that original name the child's middle name. Myra Stockdale said that she kept her daughter's Russian name "especially because it wasn't such a strange name. It was important. She had that name for two years. It was all she had. And I was just happy that it was such an easy name."

Several parents who chose to change their child's name selected a "Russian-sounding" name. The fact that many Russian origin names are either popular in the United States or are similar to names used by white Americans made the keeping of the birth name feasible for these mothers.

While culture keeping was reported to be an important aspect of China-adoptive mothering, only 19 percent decided to keep their child's given Chinese name. Mothers largely decided against keeping the Chinese name because they thought it would be too difficult for others to pronounce. They justified their decisions by arguing that the names were not *really* their children's given names (i.e., from their birth parents) but rather names doled out indiscriminately at the orphanage. One mother created first names for her daughters using part of their Chinese given names; Lorraine Burg chose "a name that was sort of signified as being an Asian name" (but not a Chinese name), as did several other mothers. The majority of parents, however, gave their child a Western first name that was often a family name or somehow connected to a specific family member (such as using the first letter of a deceased relative's name). The majority of women then kept some part of the Chinese given name as the child's middle name. In this way, mothers intended for their child to be connected to their two family histories: the history of their adoptive family/nation and the history of their birth family/nation. But in day-to-day life, only the first name of the child was generally used.

Comparing the naming practices of these two groups sheds light on the complexity of ways mothers position themselves and their children regarding birth culture. The mothers who adopted from Russia chose overwhelmingly not to practice birth culture, yet many wanted to signal the "Russian-ness" of their children in naming—a relatively simple and innocuous way to signal ethnicity, as many Russian origin names (Alex, for example) are popular among white Americans. The mothers with children from China displayed deeper commitments to birth culture, yet most changed the names of their children to Western ones that did not reflect their Chinese ethnic background.

The mothers were very clear about the reception that certain ethnically marked names would have in their communities. Names that were deemed "too Russian" ("Boris" or "Egor," for example) or "too Chinese" (such as "Xiaomei") were ruled out for fear of pronunciation problems, negative connotations, and ridicule. Neither group of women wanted ethnic identity or its related activities to impinge upon other people's acceptance of their children in the United States.

It is here that naming points to important issues of how and when and *with whom* ethnicity is operationalized by these women. Naming takes place in the context of the lives of these mothers: white, middle-class lives that, despite the "transgressive" nature of their family form, allow for very little contact across race and class. The mothers were concerned about their children having names that were "too ethnic" because they envisioned lives for their children that would also be based in white, middle-class communities. Casual observance of the naming practices of other racial and ethnic groups—later-generation Asian Americans, for example—can be seen to follow similar patterns, in which "ethnically marked" names lose popularity to be replaced by more mainstream American ones.

Naming speaks to the boundaries of culture keeping and to the limits of the representational progressive nature of these families. International-adoptive families are assumed to be on the cutting edge of race relations, but middle-class whiteness continues to profoundly shape their lived experiences. This can be seen in the people with whom the families in my study chose to engage with in performing culture keeping. The China-adoptive mothers I interviewed did not look to Chinese or Asian American mothers as role models for how to raise their children, nor did they see themselves as connected to earlier international-adoptive mothers (with children from Korea, for example) or interracial (biological) families. Rather, they saw their families as a distinct group demarcated along the lines of nonbiological kinship, interraciality (specifically white/Chinese), and "Chinese-ness." They considered themselves "pioneers" when it came to raising their daughters. Priscilla Anderson spoke of her cohort of China-adoptive mothers as "trailblazers": "There aren't that many older kids. So we don't know how it is going to work out. We are just kind of feeling our way along."

Middle-class whiteness deeply shaped the choices women with children from Russia made as well. Women who did practice culture keeping had deep commitments to facilitating Russian connections for their children, but they largely did not attempt to make connections across ethnicity, immigrant status, or class in order to engage with the Russian community. Other Russia-adoptive mothers chose not to engage in culture keeping because of the threat that it represented to the racial privilege enjoyed by their children. They gave low priority to culture keeping out of a desire to protect their children from stigma.

By highlighting shared racial identity, these women hoped to facilitate quasi-biological privilege for their families. Still others chose not to engage with birth culture as they too were concerned about the challenge to quasi-biological privilege that culture keeping would have entailed. Although they spoke of the importance of multiculturalism, these mothers avoided culture keeping because engagement with Russian culture would have highlighted to their families and the larger world that they and their children were not biologically related.

While living as adoptive mothers allowed the women in my sample to confront racial ideologies in new ways, this did not necessarily translate into deep seismic shifts in their own racial thinking. Rather, adoption made visible and then solidified the women's racial ideologies: those who had progressive politics around race prior to adoption had them reinforced through international-adoptive parenting. Those who had more conservative views around race were more prone to adopt monoracially from Russia or to espouse a colorblind orientation in raising their Chinese children.

Cross-racial or cross-class contacts that did occur took place within a distinctly middle-class context, namely consumerism. Some participants hired Chinese or Russian women as nannies for their children or as language and culture teachers; they attended presentations by Chinese or Russian adults at FCC or FRUA events; mothers bought trinkets sold by Russian or Chinese women at cultural fairs; and families would frequent Chinese or (much more rarely) Russian restaurants. By participating in culture keeping in these ways, these women were expressing *social class* as well as familial identities (Anagnost 2000). As middle-class childrearing largely centers on concerted cultivation (Lareau 2003), it makes sense that culture keeping too would have an emphasis on activities purchased, organized, and overseen by adults. These types of interactions, however, in which white mothers purchase a neatly packaged Russian or Chinese culture for their children, do little to expand traditional racial or class-based relationships.

Expanding Definitions of the Family and of Kinship

Culture keeping efforts are largely informed by the desire to negotiate the gap between the dominant normative ideology of the "American Family" (i.e., white, middle-class, heterosexual parents with biological children) and the actual lived experiences of people in diverse family forms. International-adoptive mothers confronted the ideology of the "American Family" through parenting their children. Adopting internationally deeply impacted mothers' understandings of kinship as women experienced nonbiological kinship directly. Through raising their children, the women in this study developed an understanding of family that expanded the definition beyond biological connection to include specific activities as a basis for kinship.

The concept of "kinwork" is helpful here in understanding the shift in women's thinking about kinship. Kinwork refers to the labor needed to sustain family life, to connect members, to pass on family traditions, and to celebrate holidays (di Leonardo 1984 and 1987; Stack and Burton 1993). Kinwork is distinctive from housework and includes the "conception, maintenance, and ritual celebration of cross-household kin ties" (di Leonardo 1987, 420). According to Michaela di Leonardo, "the work of kinship" includes a range of activities such as "visits, letters, presents, cards, and telephone calls to kin; services, commodities, and money exchanged between kin; and the organization of holiday gatherings. It also includes the mental or administrative labor of the creation and maintenance of fictive kin ties, decisions to intensify or neglect ties, and the responsibility for monitoring and taking part in mass media and folk discourse concerning family and kinship" (1984, 194).

Carol Stack and Linda Burton conceptualize kinwork as "the consequence of culturally constructed family obligations defined by economic, social, physical, and psychological family needs" (1993, 409). I see as part of kinwork the reflection and labor needed to negotiate various ideologies and understandings of kinship within the context of day-to-day family life. In other words, how people construct lives together as families is influenced not only by hegemonic ideologies of kinship, but also by structural factors that make the realization of that family life possible. Popular ideas on what makes a "good family," a "good mother," what children and parents need, and what makes for a healthy family life shift culturally and historically. They also vary at the individual and class level, depending on one's family situation and ability to meet those goals.

Culture keeping can be seen as a form of kinwork in that many women with children adopted from abroad see culture keeping as a distinct mothering duty and one that helps to fulfill their obligations to meet the psychological needs of their children. They engage in a good deal of mental and physical labor in thinking about, planning, and executing culture keeping for their children. The class and race privilege enjoyed by these women allow for a particular kind of culture keeping: one based largely on commodities and consumerism. While culture keeping, especially among women with children from China, also occurs in the context of adoption groups, membership in those groups and participation in their activities (e.g., "culture days" with entrance fees, reunions on Cape Cod, "mothers' night out" dinners, Chinese dance lessons) requires a level of disposable income congruent with the middle-class.

Culture keeping can also be seen as kinwork in that it is understood by mothers to be a form of connecting their children to fictive kin. As detailed in earlier chapters, women who engage in culture keeping see other children from China (or sometimes Russia) as kin to their own children. They use kinship terms when talking about those connections. They contribute time, money, and mental effort to sustain those ties for their children. In this way, the idea of "family" itself can therefore be seen to shift with international adoption. Not only are these families based on nonbiological kinship, but they encourage a type of kinship beyond the nuclear family—one that includes other adopted children and adoptive families.

Paradoxically, however, this shift in the understanding of kinship to include those outside of the legally defined family actually reinforces the idea that the family is a racial unit. The children are seen to be "like family" because they share a racial, ethnic, and national origin in addition to the shared experience of international adoption. Mothers want to engage in culture keeping with other families who match theirs as closely as possible along the lines of race, ethnicity, and even the region of the country from which they adopted or the orphanage in which their children spent their early lives. In this fictive kinship among adopted children, biological connection—the idea of race equaling family and family equaling race—is reinforced. Therefore, rather than adoption expanding ideologies of the family as a racial unit, expansions in nonbiological kinship within international adoptive families can be seen actually to reinscribe racialized kinship.

Among the many challenges parenting has brought to the lives of contemporary international adoptive mothers is a heightened sense of their positioning vis-à-vis the meaning of family and race. Across both families who adopted from China and from Russia, whiteness took on a particular importance when it was challenged by nonbiological kinship and by interraciality. Whiteness and white privilege both give structure to race in the United States and are invisible to those they benefit. Whiteness became visible to the mothers in my study when they adopted across ethnicity and kinship. Through adopting internationally, these women became consciously "raced"— consciously white—even as their families lost biological white privilege. This increased visibility, however, created an anxiety centering on that lost privilege that ran across the two groups of women. This anxiety was displayed in a focus on finding a "correct" balance between emphasizing birth culture and (adoptive) family, between "American-ness" and "Chinese-ness" or "Russian-ness," and between whiteness cast as normalcy and culture cast as difference. This anxiety reveals how race and ethnicity continue to play salient roles in how "family" is conceived. The culture keeping of international-adoptive mothers, therefore, reflects the more general ways in which ideologies of race, ethnicity, and kinship continue to shape interactions between people in the United States defined as different from one another.

Notes

Chapter 1

1. These types of arranged trips are not exclusive to the adoption community. They are popular, for example, among second- (and later-) generation Korean and Chinese youth (see Kibria 2002a, 2002b; Louie 2002, 2004).
2. Race and ethnicity were self-reported. Social class was determined using a combination of income, education, occupation, and self-identification.

Chapter 2

1. According to Roland G. Fryer Jr., "Interracial marriages account for approximately 1 percent of white marriages, 5 percent of black marriages, and 14 percent of Asian marriages" (2007, 72).
2. In contrast to this problematic framing of the adoption industry is writing that poses these placements as universally good. For example, a good deal of the published scholarly work on transracial and international adoption (e.g., Altstein and Simon 1991; Bartholet 1999; Simon and Altstein 1992)—especially that which has been written by adoptive parents—is largely uncritical of the process of adoption itself, seeing it as a win-win situation with parentless children and childless/child-needy adults finding each other.
3. During and following the Seoul Olympics of 1988, the Korean government began to restrict international adoption "at

least partially in response to media criticisms of the Korean 'export' of abandoned children and a sense of national pride" (Freundlich 2000, 93; Hübinette 2004).

4. In 2006, Guatemala surpassed Russia as the second most popular adoption program. However, in 2007, the Guatemala program was severely curtailed, and later even temporarily halted, as the Guatemalan government investigated irregularities in the adoption industry. Since April 2008, the U.S. Department of State has implemented legislation in line with the *Hague Convention on Protection of Children and Co-operation in Respect of Intercountry Adoption* (the Convention). As such, the United States has not issued immigrant visas for adopted Guatemalan children because Guatemala "has not yet established the regulations and infrastructure necessary to meet its obligations under the Convention" (Bureau of Consular Affairs 2008). Because of these changes, Russia may again reclaim the slot of the second most popular adoption program. For a breakdown of all international adoptions by country of origin, see Bureau of Consular Affairs 2008.

5. We do not have exact figures on the gender composition of children in state care in China, but it is widely understood that the number of girls heavily outweigh the number of boys for the reasons explored in this section.

6. Enforcement of these policies "can involve monitoring households' reproductive behavior, 'persuasion,' at times spilling over into direct coercion, stiff, escalating fines, and sterilization for "over-quota births" (Johnson et al. 1998). Couples in China must receive permission to give birth, and "unofficial" pregnancies are sometimes penalized with forced abortion (Li 1995). These state regulations police reproduction to varying degrees depending upon locale (Rojewski and Rojewski 2001). Couples who reside in urban areas or surrounding regions are subjected to a strict one-child policy "unless they belong to an ethnic minority or live in an exceptionally impoverished area" (Feng 2005, 3). Couples who live in regions of the country that house large numbers of ethnic minorities are allowed two or even three children. However, the

majority of couples (54 percent) are allowed only two children if the first is a girl (Feng 2005).

7. The one-son/two-child policy applied to the majority of Chinese families is indicative of a cultural preference for sons. Sons not only carry on the family name and provide much-needed assistance with manual labor but are given the familial obligation of providing care for elderly parents (Anagnost 2004; Johnson et al. 1998). In a country such as China where "there are no equivalents of social security pension programs," many couples feel the need to bear at least one son in order to secure care in old age (Tessler, Gamache, and Liu 1999, 85). Girls are not unwanted in China, however. Indicative of a desire for girls is the fact that first-born children who are girls are often kept. It is second or third daughters that are most often abandoned (Johnson 2004).

8. As Harwin discusses in *Children of the Russian State: 1917–95,* there was an agency, "The Rights of the Child," that was "to be Russia's official authorized government agency regulating all aspects of intercountry adoption." The Ministry of Education shut the agency down, however, following "allegations of profiteering" (1996, 144).

9. Medical experts and some demographers frame much contemporary infertility as rooted in delayed childbearing resulting from career-minded women (see, for example, Bewley, Davies, and Braude 2005; Martin 2000). This framing not only blames women for their infertility but casts it as a recent phenomenon. However, as journalist Liza Mundy notes, "Contrary to popular belief, female infertility is not a new condition that has been inflicted as punishment on career women who have dallied overlong in fulfilling their reproductive duty. Historically, and today, female infertility often results from tubal scarring, the result of pelvic infections that can be due to any number of causes, including sexually transmitted diseases but also childbirth itself" (2007, 27). Infertility rates do rise, of course, with increased age.

10. The names of study participants and their children have been changed to protect their privacy.

11. According to the CDC (2003), success rates are higher now, estimated in the low twentieth percentile.

12. An exception to this is the discourse found in Christian-based adoption.

13. Although international adoption was the preferred form of adoption for the women in this study, it is important to note that domestic adoptions (including stepparent adoptions) are more prevalent in the United States. According to data from the 2000 census, only 12.5 percent of all adopted children in the country (of all ages) are foreign-born (Kreider 2003). The numbers of foreign placements are on the rise; however, when compared to all adoptions in the United States (including the adoption of stepchildren), they constitute a smaller portion than domestic placements.

14. Older child adoptions from China and Russia do occur. I specifically recruited participants for my study who had adopted infants or toddlers, however, as the literature on older child adoptions points to specific issues and concerns that were not central to my research interests.

15. As reported earlier, it is estimated that 98 percent of the children adopted internationally from China are girls. There was one mother in the study, however, who was referred to and did adopt a boy from China.

16. According to *Adoptive Families Magazine,* roughly half of the children currently adopted from Russia are boys (*www. adoptivefamilies.com/russia_adoption.php*).

17. This is not to discount serious medical and cognitive issues faced by some adoptees. One study on the medical outcomes of 179 Russian adoptees found a variety of issues faced by the children. The more prevalent of these included intestinal parasites (37.2 percent), vision problems (30.3 percent), speech disorder/language delay (27 percent), developmental delay (24 percent), and ADD/ADHD (30.2 percent) (Gunnar et al. n.d.).

18. The "red thread of adoption" is very popular among China-adoptive parents and has become an important image for representing international adoption from China. As such, it has also become highly commodified. You can purchase almost any

family- or child-related item (such as photo albums, t-shirts, bibs, onesies, teddy bears, clocks, messenger bags, or aprons) embossed with an image of a red thread. There is also an expanding list of adoption blogs with the phrase "red thread" in their titles.

Chapter 3

1. This is also visible among people of color who do not share an ethnic heritage. People defined racially as black, for example, have varying experiences in the labor market depending on employers' interpretations of their ethnic backgrounds and nationalities (Waters 1999).

Chapter 4

1. The term "gotcha day" has been problematized by adult adoptees who argue that it trivializes the importance of the events surrounding adoption, is "parent-centered" and "smacks of acquiring a possession" (Moline 2008).
2. I thank Sara Dorow for our conversations about differences in China-adoptive communities that helped me to articulate this argument.
3. I purposely did not recruit participants through FCC because I wanted a range of culture keeping perspectives included. However, an ad for the study I had placed with a more general adoption organization was picked up by an FCC electronic mailing list. Roughly 38 percent of the participants in my study learned of my research project through the list, and nearly all of the China-adoptive mothers who spoke with me were members (at one time or another) of FCC.
4. Race, class, and biological privilege converge here. This is visible in the ways that poor and working class whites are culturally marginalized. A good example of this is the popular use of the term "white trash," which "helps to solidify for the middle and upper classes a sense of cultural and intellectual superiority" over poor whites (Wray and Newitz 1997, 1).
5. Statistics regarding the demographic make-up of FRUA, in terms of single vs. married parents, are unavailable.

Chapter 5

1. This "blind spot" in thinking about race and families can even be seen in professional adoption literature. For example, one such article notes, "The very nature of the differential racial characteristics between parent and children typically eliminates the possibility of the children 'passing' for being biological offspring and makes the acknowledgement of the adoption forthright" (Trolley et al. 1995, 467).

2. Qualitative differences exist in the terms "multiracial," "interracial," "biracial," "mixed race," and "transracial." "Interracial couple" refers to adults of two different races and "multiracial" person (biracial and mixed race having gone out of vogue) would refer to the biological child of their coupling. "Transracial" is commonly used in the context of adoption and refers to a child of one race being adopted by an adult(s) of another race (Dalmage 2007). I use the term "interracial families" as an umbrella term to encompass families in which two or more members, including children, can be classified as belonging to different races.

3. I thank Kimberly McClain DaCosta for our conversation that helped me to clarify this point.

References

Agger, Ben. 1989. *Fast Capitalism: A Critical Theory of Significance.* Champaign: University of Illinois Press.

———. 2004. *Speeding Up Fast Capitalism: Cultures, Jobs, Families, Schools, Bodies.* Boulder: Paradigm Publishers.

Agger, Ben, and Beth Anne Shelton. 2007. *Fast Families, Virtual Children.* Boulder: Paradigm Publishers.

Alba, Richard. 1990. *Ethnic Identity: The Transformation of White America.* New Haven: Yale University Press.

Altstein, Howard, and Rita J. Simon, eds. 1991. *Intercountry Adoption: A Multinational Perspective.* Westport, CT: Praeger.

Anagnost, Ann. 2000. "Scenes of Misrecognition: Maternal Citizenship in the Age of Transnational Adoption." *Positions: East Asia Cultures Critique* 8:389–421.

———. 2004. "Maternal Labor in a Transnational Circuit." In Taylor, Layne, and Wozniak, 139–67.

Andersen, Margaret L., and Patricia Hill Collins. 1992. Preface to *Race, Class, and Gender,* edited by Margaret L. Andersen and Patricia Hill Collins. Belmont, CA: Wadsworth.

ARO (Assistance to Russian Orphans). 2005. "Questions and Answers: Russians Orphan Epidemic." *www.aro.ru/gate/doc_files/eng_orphepi.pdf*

Azoulay, Katya Gibel. 1997. *Black, Jewish, and Interracial: It's Not the Color of Your Skin but the Race of Your Kin, and Other Myths of Identity.* Durham: Duke University Press.

Bagley, Chris. 1993. *International and Transracial Adoption: A*

Mental Health Perspective. Brookfield, VT: Ashgate Publishing Company.

Banks-Wallace, JoAnne, and Lennette Parks. 2001. " 'So That Our Souls Don't Get Damaged': The Impact of Racism on Maternal Thinking and Practice Related to the Protection of Daughters." *Issues in Mental Health Nursing* 22:77–98.

Barth, Fredrick. 1994. "Enduring and Emerging Issues in the Analysis of Ethnicity." In *The Anthropology of Ethnicity: Beyond Ethnic Groups and Boundaries,* edited by Hans Vermeulen and Cora Govers. Amsterdam: Het Spinhuis.

Bartholet, Elizabeth. 1999. *Family Bonds: Adoption, Infertility and the New World of Child Production.* Boston: Beacon Press.

Bates, J. Douglas. 1993. *Gift Children: A Story of Race, Family, and Adoption in a Divided America.* New York: Ticknor and Fields.

Batson, Christie D., Zhenchao Qian, and Daniel T. Lichter. 2006. "Interracial and Intraracial Patterns of Mate Selection among American's Diverse Black Populations." *Journal of Marriage and Family* 68:658–72.

Becker, Gay, and Robert D. Nachtigall. 1991. "Ambiguous Responsibility in the Doctor-Patient Relationship: The Case of Infertility." *Social Science and Medicine* 32 (8): 875–85.

————. " 'Born to Be a Mother': The Cultural Construction of Risk in Infertility Treatment in the U.S." *Social Science and Medicine* 39 (4): 507–18.

Bewley, Susan, Melanie Davies, and Peter Braude. 2005. "Which Career First? The Most Secure Age for Childbearing Remains 20–35." *British Medical Journal* 331:588–89.

Binder, Amy. 1999. "Friend and Foe: Boundary Work and Collective Identity in the Afrocentric and Multicultural Curriculum Movements in American Public Education." In *The Cultural Territories of Race: Black and White Boundaries,* edited by Michele Lamont, 221–48. Chicago: University of Chicago Press.

Bishoff, Tonya, and Jo Rankin, eds. 1997. *Seeds from a Silent Tree: An Anthology by Korean Adoptees.* San Diego: Pandal Press.

Beoku-Betts, Josephine A. 1995. "We Got Our Way of Cooking Things: Women, Food, and Preservation of Cultural Identity among the Gullah." *Gender and Society* 9 (5): 535–55.

Berbrier, Mitch. 2007. "The Diverse Construction of Race and Ethnicity." In *The Handbook of Constructionist Research,* edited by James A. Holstein and Jaber F. Gubrium, 567–91. New York: Guilford Press.

Briggs, Laura. 2005. "Communities Resisting Interracial Adoption: The Indian Child Welfare Act and the NABSW Statement of 1972." Paper presented at the ASAIK Conference on Adoption and Culture, Tampa.

Bureau of Consular Affairs. 2008a. "Statistics: Immigrant Visas Issued to Orphans Coming to U.S." Washington, DC: U.S. Department of State. *www.travel.state.gov/family/adoption/stats/stats_451.html.*

———. 2008b. "Warning: Adoptions Initiated in Guatemala on or after April 1, 2008." Washington, DC: U.S. Department of State. *www.travel.state.gov/family/adoption/country/country_4198.html.*

Bush, Melanie E. L. 2004. *Breaking the Code of Good Intentions: Everyday Forms of Whiteness.* Lanham, MD: Rowman and Littlefield Publishers.

Carothers, Suzanne. 1998. "Catching Sense: Learning from Our Mothers to Be Black and Female." In Hansen and Garey, 315–27.

Carp, E. Wayne. 1998. *Family Matters: Secrecy and Disclosure in the History of Adoption.* Cambridge: Harvard University Press.

———. 2002. "Introduction: A Historical Overview of American Adoption." In *Adoption in America: Historical Perspectives,* edited by E. Wayne Carp, 1–26. Ann Arbor: University of Michigan Press.

Centers for Disease Control. 1997. "1995 Assisted Reproductive Technology Success Rates. National Summary and Fertility Clinic Reports, Volume 1—Eastern United States." Atlanta: CDC. Available at *www.cdc.gov/ART/ArchivedARTPDFs/95eastern.pdf.*

———. 2003. *2003 Assisted Reproductive Technology Report.* Available at *www.cdc.gov/ART/ART2003/index.htm.*

Children's Hope International. n.d. "Adoption Guide." St. Louis: Children's Hope International Adoption Agency. *adopt.childrenshope.net.*

Childs, Erica Chito. 2005. *Navigating Interracial Borders: Black-White Couples and Their Social Worlds.* New Brunswick: Rutgers University Press.

Christian World Adoption. 2007. "Russian Adoption." *www.cwa.org/russia-adoption.htm.*

Collins, Patricia Hill. 1990. *Black Feminist Thought: Knowledge, Consciousness, and the Politics of Empowerment.* Boston: Unwin Hyman.

———. 1991. "The Meaning of Motherhood in Black Culture and Black Mother-Daughter Relationships." In *Double Stitch: Black Women Write about Mothers and Daughters,* edited by Patricia Bell Scott and Beverly Guy-Sheftall, 42–60. Boston: Beacon Press.

———. 1994. "Shifting the Center: Race, Class, and Feminist Theorizing about Motherhood." In *Mothering: Ideology, Experience and Agency,* edited by Evelyn Nakano Glenn, Grace Chang, and Linda Rennie Forcey, 45–65. New York: Routledge.

———. 1998. "It's All in the Family: Intersections of Gender, Race, and Nation." *Hypatia* 13 (3): 62–82.

Conn, Peter J. 1996. *Pearl S. Buck: A Cultural Biography.* Cambridge, UK: Cambridge University Press.

Corbin, Juliet, and Anselm Strauss. 1990. "Grounded Theory Research: Procedures, Canons, and Evaluative Criteria." *Qualitative Sociology* 13 (1): 3–21.

Cornell, Stephen. 1988. "The Transformations of the Tribe: Organization and self- concept in Native American Ethnicities." *Ethnic and Racial Studies* 11 (1): 27–47.

Cornell, Stephen, and Douglas Hartmann. 1998. *Ethnicity and Race: Making Identities in a Changing World.* Thousand Oaks, CA: Pine Forge Press.

Cox, Caroline. 1991. *Trajectories of Despair: Misdiagnosis and Maltreatment of Soviet Orphans.* Binz, Switzerland: Christian Solidarity International.

Cox, Susan Soon-Keum, ed. 1999. *Voices from Another Place: A Collection of Works from a Generation Born in Korea and Adopted to Other Countries.* St. Paul: Yeong and Yeong Book Company.

DaCosta, Kimberly McClain. 2004. "All in the Family: The Familial Roots of Racial Division." In Dalmage 2004, 19–41.

Dalmage, Heather M. 2000. *Tripping on the Color Line: Black-White Multiracial Families in a Racially Divided World.* New Brunswick: Rutgers University Press.

———, ed. 2004. *The Politics of Multiracialism: Challenging Racial Thinking.* Albany: State University of New York Press.

———. 2007. "Interracial Couples, Multiracial People, and the Color Line in Adoption." In *Adoptive Families in a Diverse Society,* edited by Katarina Wegar, 210–24. New Brunswick: Rutgers University Press.

Davis, F. James. 1991. *Who is Black? One Nation's Definition.* University Park: The Pennsylvania State University Press.

de Beauvoir, Simone. 1984. *The Second Sex.* Harmondsworth, UK: Penguin.

DeVault, Marjorie L. 1991. *Feeding the Family: The Social Organization of Caring as Gendered Work.* Chicago: University of Chicago Press.

———. 1995. "Ethnicity and Expertise: Racial-Ethnic Knowledge in Sociological Research." *Gender and Society* 9 (5): 612–31.

di Leonardo, Micaela. 1984. *The Varieties of Ethnic Experience: Kinship, Class, and Gender among California Italian-Americans.* Ithaca: Cornell University Press.

———. 1987. "The Female World of Cards and Holidays: Women, Families, and the Work of Kinship." *Signs* 12 (3): 440–53.

Dorow, Sara K. 2006a. *Transnational Adoption: A Cultural Economy of Race, Gender, and Kinship.* New York: New York University Press.

———. 2006b. "Racialized Choices: Chinese Adoption and the 'White Noise' of Blackness." *Critical Sociology* 32 (2–3): 357–79.

Drzewiecka, Jolanta A., and Kathleen Wong. 1999. "The Dynamic Construction of White Ethnicity in the Context of Transnational Cultural Formations." In *Whiteness: The Social Communication of Identity,* edited by Thomas K. Nakayama and Judith Martin, 198–216. Newbury Park, CA: Sage.

Erichsen, Jean Nelson, and Heino Erichsen. 2003. *How to Adopt Internationally: A Guide for Agency-Directed and Independent Adoptions.* Fort Worth: Mesa House Publishing.

Evan B. Donaldson Adoption Institute. 2007. "International Adoption Facts." *www.adoptioninstitute.org/FactOverview/ international.html.*

Evans, Karin. 2000. *The Lost Daughters of China: Abandoned Girls, Their Journey to America, and the Search for a Missing Past.* New York: Tarcher Putnam.

Fanshel, David. 1972. *Far From the Reservation: The Transracial Adoption of American Indian Children.* Metuchen, NJ: Scarecrow Press.

Feliciano, Cynthia. 2001. "Assimilation or Enduring Racial Boundaries? Generational Differences in Intermarriage Among Asians and Latinos in the United States." *Race and Society* 4:27–45.

Feng, Wang. 2005. "Can China Afford to Continue Its One-Child Policy?" *Asia Pacific Issues* 77:1–12.

Ferber, Abby L. 2004. "Defending the Creation of Whiteness: White Supremacy and the Threat of Interracial Sexuality." In Dalmage 2004, 43–57.

Ferguson, Susan J., ed. 2008. *Mapping the Social Landscape: Readings in Sociology.* Boston: McGraw-Hill

Fox, Greer Litton. 1999. "Families in the Media: Reflections on the Public Scrutiny of Private Behavior." *Journal of Marriage and the Family* 61:821–30.

Foucault, Michel. 1977/1995. *Discipline and Punish: The Birth of the Prison.* New York: Vintage Books.

Frankenberg, Ruth. 1993. *White Women, Race Matters: The Social Construction of Whiteness.* Minneapolis: University of Minnesota Press.

Franklin, Lynn C. 1998. *May the Circle Be Unbroken: An Intimate Journey into the Heart of Adoption.* New York: Harmony Books.

Freundlich, Madelyn. 2000. *The Role of Race, Culture, and National Origin in Adoption.* Washington, DC: Child Welfare League of America.

Fryer, Roland G. Jr. 2007. "Guess Who's Been Coming to Dinner? Trends in Interracial Marriage over the 20th Century." *Journal of Economic Perspectives* 21 (2): 71–90.

Gans, Herbert. 1979. "Symbolic Ethnicity: The Future of Ethnic

Groups and Cultures in America." *Ethnic and Racial Studies* 2:1–19.

Garey, Anita Ilta. 1995. "Constructing Motherhood on the Night Shift: 'Working Mothers' as 'Stay-at-Home Moms.' " *Qualitative Sociology* 18 (4): 415–37.

Garey, Anita Ilta, and Karen V. Hansen. 1998. "Analyzing Families with a Feminist Sociological Imagination." In Hansen and Garey, xv–xxi.

Glenn, Evelyn Nakano. 1986. *Issei, Nisei, Warbride: Three Generations of Japanese American Women in Domestic Service.* Philadelphia: Temple University Press.

Glazer, Barry, and Anselm Strauss. 1967. *The Discovery of Grounded Theory.* Chicago: Aldine Publishing.

Goffman, Erving. 1963. *Stigma: Notes on the Management of a Spoiled Identity.* New York: Simon and Schuster.

Gordon, Linda. 1999. *The Great Arizona Orphan Abduction.* Cambridge: Harvard University Press.

Gunnar, Megan R., Wendy Hellerstedt, Harold Grotevant, Dana E. Johnson, and Richard M. Lee. n.d. "Outcome of Russian Adoptions." International Adoption Project: University of Minnesota. Available at *www.childrenshomeadopt.org.*

Hansen, Karen V. 2001. "Class Contingencies in Networks of Care for School-Aged Children," Working Paper Series, No. 27, Center for Working Families, University of California, Berkeley, May. *wfnetwork.bc.edu/berkeley/papers/27.pdf*

———. 2005. *Not-so-nuclear Families: Class, Gender, and Networks of Care.* New Brunswick: Rutgers University Press.

Hansen, Karen V., and Anita Ilta Garey, eds. 1998. *Families in the U.S.: Kinship and Domestic Politics.* Philadelphia: Temple University Press.

Harwin, Judith. 1996. *Children of the Russian State: 1917–95.* Brookfield, VT: Ashgate Publishing Company.

Hays, Sharon. 1996. *The Cultural Contradictions of Motherhood.* New Haven: Yale University Press.

Herman, Ellen. 2005. "Transracial Adoptions." *The Adoption History Project. darkwing.uoregon.edu/~adoption/topics/ transracialadoption.htm.*

Herrmann, Kenneth J., Jr., and Barbara Kasper. 1992. "International Adoption: The Exploitation of Women and Children." *Affilia* 7 (1): 45–58.

Hochschild, Arlie Russell. 1997. *The Time Bind: When Work Becomes Home and Home Becomes Work.* New York: Metropolitan Books.

Hollinger, Joan Heifetz. 1998. *A Guide to The Multiethnic Placement Act of 1994 As Amended by the Interethnic Adoption Provisions of 1996.* Washington, DC: American Bar Association Center on Children and the Law. *www.acf.hhs.gov/programs/cb/pubs/mepa94.*

hooks, bell. 1992. *Black Looks: Race and Representation.* Boston: South End Press.

Hübinette, Tobias. 2004. "Korean Adoption History." In *Community 2004: Guide to Korea for Overseas Adopted Koreans,* edited by Eleana Kim. Seoul: Overseas Koreans Foundation. *www.tobiashubinette.se/adoption_history.pdf*

Ignatiev, Noel. 1996. *How the Irish Became White.* New York: Routledge.

Ishizawa, Hiromi, Catherine T. Kenney, Kazuyo Kubo, and Gillian Stevens. 2006. "Constructing Interracial Families Through Intercountry Adoption." *Social Science Quarterly* 87 (5): 1207–24.

Jacobs, Jerry A., and Teresa G. Labov. 2002. "Gender Differentials in Intermarriage Among Sixteen Race and Ethnic Groups." *Sociological Forum* 17 (4): 621–46.

Jacobson, Matthew Frye. 1998. *Whiteness of a Different Color: European Immigrants and the Alchemy of Race.* Cambridge: Harvard University Press.

Johnson, Kay. 2004. *Wanting a Daughter, Needing a Son: Abandonment, Adoption, and Orphanage Care in China.* St. Paul: Yeong and Yeong Book Company.

Johnson, Kay, Huang Banghan, and Wang Liyao. 1998. "Infant Abandonment and Adoption in China." *Population and Development Review* 24 (3): 469–502.

Johnston, Patricia Irwin. 1992. *Adopting After Infertility.* Indianapolis: Perspectives Press.

Kenny, Lorraine Delia. 2000a. *Daughters of Suburbia: Growing Up*

White, Middle Class, and Female. New Brunswick: Rutgers University Press.

———. 2000b. "Doing My Homework: The Autoethnography of a White Teenage Girl." In *Racing Research, Researching Race: Methodological Dilemmas in Critical Race Studies,* edited by France Winddance Twine and Jonathan W. Warren, 111–33. New York: New York University Press.

Kibria, Nazli. 1997. "The Concept of 'Bicultural Families' and Its Implications for Research on Immigrant and Ethnic Families." In *Immigration and the Family: Research and Policy on U.S. Immigrants,* edited by Alan Booth, Ann C. Crouter, and Nancy Landale, 205–210. Mahwah, NJ: Lawrence Erlbaum Associates.

———. 2002a. *Becoming Asian American: Second-Generation Chinese and Korean American Identities.* Baltimore: Johns Hopkins University Press.

———. 2002b. "Of Blood, Belonging, and Homeland Trips: Transnationalism and Identity Among Second-Generation Chinese and Korean Americans." In Levitt and Waters, 295–311.

Kim, Katherin M. Flower. 2008. "Out of Sorts: Adoption and (Un) Desirable Children." In Ferguson, 393–406.

Kim, Sarah. 2007. "To Willow Janowitz: You're not alone. . . ." *Outside In . . . And Back Again,* November 13. *sarahkim. wordpress.com.*

Klose, Robert. 1999. *Adopting Alyosha: A Single Man Finds a Son in Russia.* Jackson: University Press of Mississippi.

Koh, Frances M. 1981. *Oriental Children in American Homes.* Minneapolis: East West Press.

———. 1993. *Adopted from Asia: How It Feels to Grow Up in America.* Minneapolis: East West Press.

Kreider, Rose M. 2003. "Adopted Children and Stepchildren: 2000." Census 2000 Special Report. Washington, DC: U.S. Census Bureau. *www.census.gov/prod/2003pubs/censr-6.pdf.*

Kristeva, Julia. 1991. *Strangers to Ourselves.* New York: Columbia University Press.

Lareau, Annette. 2000. "My Wife Can Tell Me Who I Know: Methodological and Conceptual Problems in Studying Fathers." *Qualitative Sociology* 23 (4): 407–33.

————. 2003. *Unequal Childhoods: Class, Race, and Family Life.*
    Berkeley: University of California Press.

Lazarre, Jane. 1996. *Beyond the Whiteness of Whiteness: Memoir of
    a White Mother of Black Sons.* Durham: Duke University Press.

Lee, Jennifer, and Frank D. Bean. 2004. "America's Changing
    Color Lines: Immigration, Race/Ethnicity, and Multiracial
    Identification." *Annual Review of Sociology* 30 (1): 221–42.

Leiter, Valerie, Jennifer Lutzy McDonald, and Heather T.
    Jacobson. 2006. "Challenges to Independent Child Citizenship:
    Immigration, Family, and the State." *Childhood: A Global
    Journal of Child Research* 13 (1): 11–27.

Levitt, Peggy, and Mary C. Waters, eds. 2002. *The Changing Face of
    Home: The Transnational Lives of the Second Generation.* New
    York: Russell Sage Foundation.

Li, Jiali. 1995. "China's One-Child Policy: How and How Well
    Has It Worked? A Case Study of Hebei Province, 1979–88."
    Population and Development Review 21 (3): 563–85.

Lieberson, Stanley, and Eleanor O. Bell. 1992. "Children's First
    Names: An Empirical Study of Social Taste." *American Journal
    of Sociology* 98 (3): 511–54.

Liem, Deanna Borshay. 2000. *First Person Plural.* San Francisco:
    National Asian American Telecommunications Association
    (NAATA).

Liu, Jihong, Ulla Larsen, and Grace Wyshak. 2004. "Factors
    Affecting Adoption in China, 1950–1987." *Population Studies* 58
    (1): 21–36.

Lifton, Betty Jean. 1987. "Brave New Baby in the Brave New
    World." *Women and Health Magazine* 13 (1–2): 149–53.

Lorber, Judith. 1995. *Paradoxes of Gender.* New Haven: Yale
    University Press.

Louie, Andrea. 2002. "Creating Histories for the Present: Second-
    Generation (Re)definitions of Chinese American Culture." In
    Levitt and Waters, 312–40.

————. 2004. *Chineseness Across Borders: Renegotiating Chinese
    Identities in China and the United States.* Durham: Duke
    University Press.

————. 2008. "Crafting 'Chinese' Identities: 'Birth Culture' and

Adoption in the Context of U.S. Multiculturalism." Paper presented at the annual meeting of the Association for Asian American Studies, Chicago.

Loux, Ann Kimble. 1997. *The Limits of Hope: An Adoptive Mother's Story.* Charlottesville: University Press of Virginia.

Lucal, Betsy. 2008. "What It Means to Be Gendered Me: Life on the Boundaries of a Dichotomous Gender System." In Ferguson, 315–30.

Luke, Carmen, and Allan Luke. 1998. "Interracial Families: Difference within Difference." *Ethnic and Racial Studies* 21 (4): 728–54.

Martin, Steven P. 2000. "Diverging Fertility Among U.S. Women Who Delay Childbearing Past Age 30." *Demography* 37 (4): 523–33

Massey, Douglas S., and Nancy A. Denton. 1993. *American Apartheid: Segregation and the Making of the Underclass.* Cambridge: Harvard University Press.

McAdoo, Harriette Pipes. 1999. Introduction to *Family Ethnicity: Strength in Diversity,* edited by Harriette Pipes McAdoo. Thousand Oaks: Sage Publications.

McBride, James. 1996. *The Color of Water: A Black Man's Tribute to His White Mother.* New York: Riverhead Books.

McCabe, Nancy. 2003. *Meeting Sophie: A Memoir of Adoption.* Columbia: University of Missouri Press.

McCall, Leslie. 2005. "The Complexity of Intersectionality." *Signs: Journal of Women in Culture and Society* 30 (3): 1771–1800.

McIntosh, Peggy. 1988. "White Privilege and Male Privilege: A Personal Account of Coming to See Correspondences through Work in Women's Studies." Working Paper 189. Wellesley, MA: Wellesley College Center for Research on Women.

McKinney, Karyn D. 2005. *Being White: Stories of Race and Racism.* New York: Routledge.

Meese, Ruth Lyn. 2005. "A Few New Children: Postinstitutionalized Children of Intercountry Adoption." *Journal of Special Education* 39 (3): 157–67.

Melosh, Barbara. 2002. *Strangers and Kin: The American Way of Adoption.* Cambridge: Harvard University Press.

Miller-Loessi, Karen, and Kilic Zeynep. 2001. "A Unique Diaspora? The Case of Adopted Girls from the People's Republic of China." *Diaspora* 10 (2): 243–60.

Modell, Judith. 1994. *Kinship with Strangers: Adoption and Interpretations of Kinship in American Culture.* Berkeley: University of California Press.

———. 2002. *A Sealed and Secret Kinship: The Culture of Policies and Practices in American Adoption.* New York: Berghahn Books.

Moline, Karen. 2008. "Get Rid of 'Gotcha.'" *Adoptive Families Magazine. www.adoptivefamilies.com/articles.php?aid=1266.*

Moosenick, Nora Rose. 2004. *Adopting Maternity: White Women Who Adopt Transracially or Transnationally.* Westport, CT: Praeger.

Moran, Rachel F. 2001. *Interracial Intimacy: The Regulation of Race and Romance.* Chicago: University of Chicago Press.

Morris, Ann. 1999. *The Adoption Experience: Families Who Give Children a Second Chance.* Philadelphia: Taylor and Francis.

Moynihan, Daniel. 1965. "The Negro Family: The Case for National Action." Washington, DC: United States Department of Labor.

Mundy, Liza. 2007. *Everything Conceivable: How Assisted Reproduction Is Changing Men, Women, and the World.* New York: Alfred A. Knopf.

Nagel, Joane. 1994. "Constructing Ethnicity: Creating and Recreating Ethnic Identity and Culture." *Social Problems* 41:152–76.

National People's Congress. 1991. "Adoption Law of the People's Republic of China. People's Republic of China." 23rd Meeting of the Standing Committee of the Seventh National People's Congress. Available at the Chinese government's official web portal, *english.gov.cn/2005–08/31/content_26770.htm.*

Newfield, Christopher, and Avery F. Gordon. 1996. "Multiculturalism's Unfinished Business." In *Mapping Multiculturalism,* edited by Christopher Newfield and Avery F. Gordon, 76–115. Minneapolis: University of Minnesota Press.

Newman, Janis Cooke. 2001. *The Russian Word for Snow: A True Story of Adoption.* New York: St. Martin's Press.

Omi, Michael, and Howard Winant. 1994. *Racial Formation in the United States: From the 1960s to the 1990s.* New York: Routledge.

Orenstein, Peggy. 2007. *Waiting for Daisy: A Tale of Two Continents, Three Religions, Five Infertility Doctors, an Oscar, an Atomic Bomb, a Romantic Night.* New York: Bloomsbury.

Page, Janice. 2004. "And Zoe Makes Three." *Boston Globe Magazine,* October 3. *www.boston.com.*

Patton, Sandra. 2000. *Birth Marks: Transracial Adoption in Contemporary America.* New York: New York University Press.

Perlmann, Joel. 2000. "Reflecting the Changing Face of America: Multiracials, Racial Classification, and American Intermarriage." In *Interracialism: Black-White Intermarriage in American History, Literature, and Law,* edited by Werner Sollors, 506–34. New York: Oxford University Press.

Pertman, Adam. 2000. *Adoption Nation: How the Adoption Revolution is Transforming America.* New York: Basic Books.

Pomerleau, Andrée, Gérard Malcuit, Jean-François Chicoine, Renée Seguin, Céline Belhumeur, Patricia Germain, Isabelle Amyot, and Gloria Jeliu. 2005. "Health Status, Cognitive and Motor Development of Young Children Adopted from China, East Asia, and Russia Across the First 6 Months After Adoption." *International Journal of Behavioral Development* 29 (5): 445–57.

Pyke, Karen. 2000. " 'The Normal American Family' as an Interpretive Structure of Family Life Among Grown Children of Korean and Vietnamese Immigrants." *Journal of Marriage and Family,* 62 (1): 240–55.

Qian, Zhenchao. 2005. "Breaking the Last Taboo: Interracial Marriage in America." *Contexts* 4 (4): 33–37.

Reddy, Maureen T. 1996. *Crossing the Color Line: Race, Parenting, and Culture.* New Brunswick: Rutgers University Press.

Register, Cheri. 1991. *Are Those Kids Yours? American Families with Children Adopted from Other Countries.* New York: Free Press.

Roberts, Dorothy. 2003. *Shattered Bonds: The Color of Child Welfare.* New York: Basic Books.

Robinson, Katy. 2002. *A Single Square Picture.* New York: Berkley.

Rothman, Barbara Katz. 2005. *Weaving a Family: Untangling Race and Adoption.* Boston: Beacon Press.

Rojewski, Jay W., and Jacy L. Rojewski. 2001. *Intercountry Adoption from China: Examining Cultural Heritage and Other Postadoption Issues.* Westport, CT: Bergin and Garvey.

Saidazimova, Gulnoza. 2005. "Russia: Boy's Death, Mother's Sentencing Lead To Appeals for Adoption Restrictions." Radio Free Europe/Radio Liberty, May 6. *www.rferl.org.*

Scroggs, Patricia Hanigan, and Heather Heitfield. 2001. "International Adopters and their Children: Birth Culture Ties." *Gender Issues* 19 (4): 3–30.

Selman, Peter. 2002. "Intercountry Adoption in the New Millennium: The 'Quiet Migration' revisited." *Population Research and Policy Review* 21:205–25.

Serbin, Lisa A. 1997. "Research on International Adoption: Implications for Developmental Theory and Social Policy." *International Journal of Behavioral Development* 20 (1): 83–92.

Shiao, Jiannbin Lee, Mia Tuan, and Elizabeth Rienzi. 2004. "Shifting the Spotlight: Exploring Race and Culture in Korean-White Adoptive Families." *Race and Society* 7 (1): 1–16.

Silverman, Arnold. 1993. "Outcomes of Transracial Adoption." *The Future of Children: Adoption.* Los Altos, CA: David and Lucile Packard Foundation.

Simon, Rita J., and Howard Altstein. 1992. *Adoption, Race, and Identity: From Infancy through Adolescence.* Westport, CT: Praeger.

Sindelar, Rita. 2004. "Negotiating Indian Identity: Native Americans and Transracial Adoption." MA thesis, Loyola University Chicago.

Sloutsky, Vladimir. 1997. "Institutional Care and Developmental Outcomes of 6- and 7- year old Children: A Contextual Perspective." *International Journal of Behavioral Development* 20 (1): 131–51.

Smith, Dorothy. 1993. "The Standard North American Family: SNAF as an Ideological Code." *Journal of Family Issues* 14 (1): 50–65.

Solinger, Rickie. 2001. *Beggars and Choosers: How the Politics of Choice Shapes Adoption, Abortion, and Welfare in the United States.* New York: Farrar, Straus, and Giroux.

Sorosky, Arthur D., Annette Baran, and Reuben Pannor. 1978. *The Adoption Triangle: The Effects of the Sealed Record on Adoptees, Birth Parents, and Adoptive Parents.* Garden City, NY: Anchor Press/Doubleday.

Stacey, Judith. 1996. *In the Name of the Family: Rethinking Family Values in the Postmodern Age.* Boston: Beacon Press.

Stack, Carol B. 1974. *All Our Kin: Strategies for Survival in a Black Community.* New York: Harper and Row.

Stack, Carol, and Linda Burton. 1993. "Kinscripts." *Journal of Comparative Family Studies* 24 (2): 157–70.

Steinberg, Gail, and Beth Hall. 2000. *Inside Transracial Adoption.* Indianapolis: Perspectives Press.

Steltzner, Donovan. 2003. "Intercountry Adoption: Toward a Regime that Recognizes the 'Best Interests' of Adoptive Parents." *Case Western Reserve Journal of International Law* 35 (1): 113–52.

Stiers, Gretchen A. 2007. "From This Day Forward: Commitment, Marriage, and Family in Lesbian and Gay Relationships." In *Shifting the Center: Understanding Contemporary Families,* edited by Susan J. Ferguson, 251–64. Boston: McGraw Hill Higher Education, third edition.

Taylor, Janelle S., Linda L. Layne, and Danielle F. Wozniak, eds. 2004. *Consuming Motherhood.* New Brunswick: Rutgers University Press.

Tessler, Richard, Gail Gamache, and Liming Liu. 1999. *West Meets East: Americans Adopt Chinese Children.* Westport, CT: Bergin and Garvey.

Townsend, Nicholas W. 2002. *The Package Deal: Marriage, Work and Fatherhood in Men's Lives.* Philadelphia: Temple University Press.

Trenka, Jane Jeong, Julia Chinyere Oparah, and Sun Yung Shin, eds. 2006. *Outsiders Within: Writing on Transracial Adoption.* Cambridge, MA: South End Press.

Trenka, Jane Jeong. 2003. *The Language of Blood: A Memoir.* St. Paul: Borealis Books.

Trolley, Barbara C., Julia Wallin, and James Hansen. 1995. "International Adoption: Issues of Acknowledgement of

Adoption and Birth Culture." *Child and Adolescent Social Work Journal* 12 (6): 465–79.

Tuan, Mia. 1998. *Forever Foreigners or Honorary Whites? The Asian Ethnic Experience Today.* New Brunswick: Rutgers University Press.

Twine, France Winddance. 1997. "Brown-Skinned White Girls: Class, Culture, and the Construction of White Identity in Suburban Communities." In *Displacing Whiteness: Essays in Social and Cultural Criticism,* edited by Ruth Frankenberg, 214–43. Durham: Duke University Press.

United Nations. 1989. "Convention on the Rights of the Child." November 20. *United Nations Treaty Series* 1577:3. New York: UN General Assembly.

U.S. Congress. 1978. *Indian Child Welfare Act.* Washington, DC: U.S. Government Printing Office.

———. 2000. *Adopted Orphans Citizenship Act and Anti-Atrocity Alien Deportation Act.* Washington, DC: U.S. Government Printing Office.

Uttal, Lynet. 1998. "Racial Safety and Cultural Maintenance: The Child Care Concerns of Employed Mothers of Color." In Hansen and Garey, 597–606.

Volkman, Toby Alice. 2003. "Embodying Chinese Culture: Transnational Adoption in North America." *Social Text* 21 (1): 29–55.

———. 2005. "Introduction: New Geographies of Kinship." In *Cultures of Transnational Adoption,* edited by Toby Alice Volkman, 1–22. Durham: Duke University Press.

Vonk, Elizabeth M. 2001. "Cultural Competence for Transracial Adoptive Parents." *Social Work* 46 (3): 246–55.

Waters, Mary C. 1990. *Ethnic Options: Choosing Identities in America.* Berkeley: University of California Press.

———. 1999. *Black Identities: West Indian Immigrant Dreams and American Realities.* Cambridge: Harvard University Press.

Weber, Mac. 1949. *The Methodology of the Social Sciences.* Blacklick, OH: Glencoe Press.

Wegar, Katarina. 1997. *Adoption, Identity, and Kinship: The Debate over Sealed Birth Records.* New Haven: Yale University Press.

West, Candace, and Don H. Zimmerman. 1987. "Doing Gender." *Gender and Society* 1 (2): 125–51.

Weston, Kath. 1991. *Families We Choose: Lesbians, Gays, Kinship.* New York: Columbia University Press.

Wildman, Stephanie M. 1996. *Privilege Revealed: How Invisible Preference Undermines America.* New York: New York University Press.

Wolff, Jana. 2000. *Secret Thoughts of an Adoptive Mother.* Honolulu: Vista Communications.

Wray, Matt, and Annalee Newitz, eds. 1997. *White Trash: Race and Class in America.* New York: Routledge.

Yngvesson, Barbara. 2004. "Going 'Home': Adoption, Exclusive Belongings, and the Mythology of Roots." In Taylor, Layne, and Wozniak, 168–86.

Zbarskaya, Irina, coordinator. 2001. "Child and Family Welfare in Russia: Trends and Indicators." Background paper prepared for UNICEF Regional Monitoring Report No. 8: A Decade of Transition. Florence, Italy: UNICEF Innocenti Research Centre. Available at *www.unicef-irc.org.*

Zelizer, Viviana A. 1985. *Pricing the Priceless Child: The Changing Social Value of Children.* Princeton: Princeton University Press.

Zeng, Y, P. Tu, B. Gu, Y Xu, B. Li, and Y. Li. 1993. "Causes and Implications of the Recent Increase in the Reported Sex Ratio at Birth in China." *Population and Development Review* 19 (1): 283–302.

Zhou, Min. 2000. "Social Capital in Chinatown: the Role of Community-Based Organizations and Families in the Adaptation of the Younger Generation." In *Contemporary Asian America: A Multidisciplinary Reader,* edited by Min Zhou and James V. Gatewood, 315–35. New York: New York University Press.

Zollar, Ann Creighton. 1985. *A Member of the Family: Strategies for Black Family Continuity.* Chicago: Nelson-Hall Publishers.

Index

abandonment of children, 77–80
  in China, 23, 76, 111–12, 179n7
  in Russia, 21–23
  and self-esteem and self-
    confidence of children,
    77–78, 139
Abramson, Rachel, 38, 43, 95, 117,
  121, 148
Acher, Carol, 80, 125, 131, 132, 160
"adopted child syndrome," 66
Adopted Orphans Citizenship Act
  (proposed), 85
adoption agencies. *See* business of
  international adoption
adoption decision. *See* decision to
  adopt
adoption groups
  and China-adoptive families,
    118–21, 142
  and interracial surveillance,
    163
  and Russia-adoptive families,
    129–32
  See also Families for Russian
    and Ukrainian Adoption
    (FRUA); Families with
    Children from China
    (FCC)

adoption medicine specialists,
  consultation with, 47
adoptive practices and trends
  in 1950s and 1960s, 3–4, 16
  in 1970s, 4, 16
  age of children for adoption,
    39
  domestic vs. international
    adoptions, 31–37, 180n13
  matching by race, ethnicity, or
    religion, 16, 165–66
  new attitudes toward
    interracial families,
    166–67
  open adoptions, 36, 92
  public surveillance of
    interracial families,
    145–63
African Americans
  avoidance of adopting black
    child, 33, 42, 44–45, 149
  fostering pride to counter
    racism, 68
  and kinship adoptions, 15
  mothers constructing safe
    environment for children,
    61–63
  and transracial adoptions,
    16–18, 150